BIBLE STUDY GUIDE

From the Bible-teaching ministry of

CHARLES R. SWINDOLL

INSIGHT FOR LIVING

Chuck graduated in 1963 from Dallas Theological Seminary, where he now serves as the school's fourth president, helping to prepare a new generation of men and women for the ministry. Chuck has served in pastorates in three states: Massachusetts, Texas, and California, including almost twenty-three years at the First Evangelical Free Church in Fullerton, California. His sermon messages have been aired over radio since 1979 as the *Insight for Living* broadcast. A best-selling author, Chuck has written numerous books and booklets on many subjects.

Based on the outlines and transcripts of Chuck's sermons, the study guide text is co-authored by Ken Gire, a graduate of Texas Christian University and Dallas Theological Seminary. He also wrote the Living Insights sections.

Editor in Chief:
Cynthia Swindoll

Typographer:
Bob Haskins

Coauthor of Text:
Ken Gire

Director, Communications Division:
Carla Beck

Assistant Editor:
Wendy Peterson

Project Manager:
Alene Cooper

Copyediting Supervisor:
Marty Anderson

Print Production Manager:
Deedee Snyder

Copy Editor:
Connie Laser

Assistant Production Manager:
John Norton

Text Designer:
Gary Lett

Printer
Sinclair Printing Company

Unless otherwise identified, all Scripture references are from the New American Standard Bible, © The Lockman Foundation 1960, 1962, 1963, 1968, 1971, 1972, 1973, 1975, 1977. Used by permission. The other translation cited is *The Living Bible* [LB].

An effort has been made to locate sources and obtain permission where necessary for the quotations used in this book. In the event of any unintentional omission, a modification will gladly be incorporated in future printings.

ISBN 0-8499-8735-0
Printed in the United States of America

CONTENTS

INTRODUCTION

It was in the 1700s that a series of revivals in the American colonies led to an awakening. The movement began in the middle colonies and soon spread north into New England and, shortly thereafter, south into the Carolinas and Georgia.

The leaders were many: Jonathan Edwards, George Whitefield, Gilbert Tennent, and several other well-known preachers, not to mention the Wesley brothers in Great Britain. They delivered strong messages of the Cross, stirring the hearts of thousands. The exciting movement came to be known as "The Great Awakening." What remarkable changes occurred as a result of God's working!

None can deny that there is the need for yet another awakening among God's people . . . a renewed appreciation for and acceptance of His grace. As grace sweeps over us, the freedom Christ promised will return and the joy of His Spirit will become evident.

The Grace Awakening is a study about freedom.

I have never delivered a series of messages that prompted more response than this one. Without question, the subject of grace—God's amazing, liberating grace—is one that people everywhere hunger to hear. Long enough has legalism held sway over God's people! There is an awakening of grace spreading across our land . . . a movement whose time has come.

What is it that causes our Lord to stoop and reach out to us in love? Grace. What is it that frees us to be all He means us to be? What is it that permits others to be who they are, even very different from us? Grace. What allows us to disagree, yet stimulates us to press on? Grace. What adds oil to the friction points of a marriage, freeing both partners from pettiness and negativism? Grace. And what gives magnetic charm to a ministry, inviting others to become a part? Again . . . grace.

Grace will conquer the things that steal the Christian's motivation: guilt and shame, legalism and negativism, petty fighting and small-minded intolerance, as well as others' expectations and self-imposed restrictions, to name only a few.

The Grace Awakening is not a series for the fainthearted. It is a bold and needed declaration for pastors, for Christian leaders, for missionaries, for young and old believers alike. I am so glad you will be traveling with us through this delightful journey. My prayer is that each study will be used of God to break the shackles, that all who listen and learn may be "free indeed." May the Spirit of God use the Word of God to show us the beauty and necessity of the grace of God.

Chuck Swindoll

PUTTING TRUTH INTO ACTION

Knowledge apart from application falls short of God's desire for His children. He wants us to apply what we learn so that we will change and grow. This study guide was prepared with these goals in mind. As you go through the following pages, we hope your desire to discover biblical truth will grow as your understanding of God's Word increases and that you will be encouraged to apply what you've learned.

To assist you in your study, we've included a section called **Living Insights** at the end of each lesson. These exercises will challenge you to study further and to think of specific ways to put your discoveries into action.

There are many ways to use this guide—in personal devotions, group studies, discussions with friends and family, and Sunday school classes. And, of course, it's an ideal study aid when you're listening to its corresponding *Insight for Living* radio series.

To benefit most from this study guide, we would encourage you to consider it a spiritual journal. That's why we've included space in the **Living Insights** for recording your thoughts and discoveries. We hope you'll return to those sections often for review and encouragement as you continue to grow in your walk with Christ.

Ken Gire

Ken Gire
Coauthor of Text
Author of Living Insights

Grace scales the wall and refuses to be restricted.

Grace lives above the demands of human opinion
and breaks free from legalistic regulations.

Grace dares us to take hold of the sledge of courage
and break through longstanding stones.

Grace invites us to chart new courses
and explore everexpanding regions,
all the while delighting in the unexpected.

While others care more about maintaining the wall
and fearing those who guard it,
grace is constantly looking for ways to freedom.

Grace wants faith to fly,
regardless of what grim-faced officials may
say or think or do.

Grace is the demonstration of Jesus' words:
"If therefore the Son shall make you free,
you shall be free indeed."

—Charles R. Swindoll
The Grace Awakening

Chapter 1

GRACE:
IT'S *REALLY* AMAZING
Selected Scriptures

In his book *The Vital Balance*, Dr. Karl Menninger discusses the negative personality. Essentially, it is a personality whose first response is to say no to everything.

To contrast this negative outlook with a positive one toward life, Menninger tells this story. One day President Thomas Jefferson and a group of other men were fording a swollen stream on horseback. A man on the bank of the river waited until several of the men crossed. Then he waved to Jefferson and asked to be taken across, and the president gladly obliged.

When the wayfarer reached the other side, one of the men asked, "Tell me, why did you select the President to ask this favor of?"

The man replied, "I didn't know he was the President. All I know is that on some faces is written the answer 'No' and on some the answer 'Yes.' His face was one of the latter."[1]

That illustration holds a powerful insight: As the face of the moon reflects the sun, so the face of a person reflects grace. Sometimes that grace is eclipsed by the sin in our life. Other times it beams full and radiant. At such shining moments we reflect a glimmer of the Lord Jesus. That's what the poorest of the poor in India's streets see when they look up at the wrinkled face of Mother Teresa. They see the eyes of Jesus, the tears of Jesus, and the smile of Jesus. They see a reflection of grace.

---

1. Karl Menninger, with Martin Mayman and Paul Pruyser, *The Vital Balance*, Viking Compass ed. (New York, N.Y.: Viking Press, 1967), pp. 204–5.

1

What do people see when they look at your face? Do they see the worries of the world etched in a wrinkled forehead and knitted brow? Do they see the harshness of the dog-eat-dog business world chiseled in a stone jaw? Do they see the frazzle of depression and fatigue scribbled in bloodshot eyes?

If they do, maybe it's time for a face-lift. Maybe it's time for God's grace to do a mighty work in your life. Grace *is* really amazing, for it will not only change the way you look at others but the way others look at you.

Grace: A Plea for Understanding

When people looked at Jesus, they saw a "yes" face, a face radiant with grace and truth (John 1:14, 16).

> For the Law was given through Moses; grace and truth were realized through Jesus Christ. (v. 17)

With the Law came bondage, but with grace comes freedom. In Christ we see grace incarnate. In every sermon He preached, in every person He healed, we see the different nuances of this glorious word *grace*.

Explanation of the Term

Nowhere in Scripture is a specific definition of grace given. The Hebrew term is *chen*, meaning "to bend or stoop." It came to mean "condescending favor." It is the kindness "shown by a superior to an inferior, and there is no obligation on the part of the superior to show this kindness."[2] This meaning is illustrated in God's speaking to Moses about Israel's inheritance of the Promised Land in Exodus 33:14–19.

> And He said, "My presence shall go with you, and I will give you rest." Then he said to Him, "If Thy presence does not go with us, do not lead us up from here. For how then can it be known that I have found favor in Thy sight, I and Thy people? Is it not by Thy going with us, so that we, I and Thy people, may be distinguished from all the other people who are upon the face of the earth?"

---

2. Norman H. Snaith, "Grace," in *A Theological Word Book of the Bible*, Macmillan Paperbacks ed., ed. Alan Richardson (New York, N.Y.: Macmillan Co., 1962), p. 100.

And the Lord said to Moses, "I will also do this thing of which you have spoken; for you have found favor in My sight, and I have known you by name." Then Moses said, "I pray Thee, show me Thy glory!" And He said, "I Myself will make all My goodness pass before you, and will proclaim the name of the Lord before you; and I will be gracious to whom I will be gracious, and will show compassion on whom I will show compassion."

As this passage indicates, grace is favor that is undeserved and unearned. It is extended fully and freely to those who won't ever be able to repay it.

Extent of the Truth

The term *grace* covers a wide range of meanings. But the common tone that resonates in them all is that of pleasantness. Grace describes the coordination and fluidity of a dancer or an athlete, a ballerina as well as a quarterback. Grace can describe a person's manners and gentility. Grace is the soothing balm that gives comfort to the downtrodden. Beautiful words are said to be words of grace. And it is upon this great theological word that our eternal destiny hangs, for the undeserved favor of God is our only hope of being accepted by Him.

Interestingly, Jesus never used the term *grace*. Instead of mouthing the word, He modeled the reality. The best definition of grace doesn't come from a dictionary, but from the pages of His own life.

Grace seeps through the text of the woman caught in adultery. It can be read between every line of every story He told. From the Good Samaritan to the story of the Prodigal Son, grace can be rubbed off the pages like newspaper ink. Even in His rebukes, grace softens every word. When He tells Martha that she is worried and bothered about so many things, we can hear the plaintive tone of tenderness in His voice (Luke 10:41).

As we align ourselves to the smooth, gilded pages of the Gospels, the rough and tattered edges of our lives stand out with glaring irregularity.

How quick we are to speak the truth, but not in love. How ready we are to rebuke, but not to restore. How eager we are to barter gossip, but not to bestow grace.

If this is true of your life, our Lord has something He wants to tell you.

3

"Do not judge lest you be judged. For in the way you judge, you will be judged; and by your standard of measure, it will be measured to you. And why do you look at the speck that is in your brother's eye, but do not notice the log that is in your own eye? Or how can you say to your brother, 'Let me take the speck out of your eye,' and behold, the log is in your own eye? You hypocrite, first take the log out of your own eye, and then you will see clearly to take the speck out of your brother's eye." (Matt. 7:1–5)

How haunting are the words of Peter at the end of his second letter: "but grow in the grace and knowledge of our Lord and Savior Jesus Christ" (3:18a). Don't write this off as a breezy "best wishes" ending, hastily scribbled before he sealed the envelope. It may be easy to grow in knowledge—any book or Bible college could help you do that. But Peter knew that to grow in grace is a graduate school assignment. Small wonder that Timothy, the freshman pastor, was instructed by his tutor to "be strong in . . . grace" (2 Tim. 2:1), for it is the only major that matters when it comes to church work.

Several Scriptural Examples

The Bible is replete with examples of God's grace, not only in the New Testament but also in the Old.

> The idea of grace more than any other idea binds the two Testaments together into a complete whole, for the Bible is the story of the saving work of God, that is, of the grace of God. Without grace, there would never have been any chosen people, any story to tell at all.[3]

In the Old Testament

When we think of the Old Testament, we think more about the justice of God than we do about His mercy. The images we conjure up are ones of fire and brimstone falling on Sodom and Gomorrah, rather than sweet manna falling from heaven to feed the children of Israel in the wilderness.

---

3. Snaith, "Grace," p. 101.

And yet, the first time the term *grace* appears is in Genesis 6:8. Here the Hebrew word *chen* is rendered "favor."

But Noah found favor in the eyes of the Lord.

In many of the Old Testament stories grace is so central to the drama that it resounds in every scene like a strong musical score. Consider Joseph's treatment of his jealous and ruthless brothers in Genesis 42–50, especially 45:1–15. Reflect on the gracious way that God dealt with the Hebrews on their way from Egypt to Canaan in the books of Exodus and Numbers. Meditate on the deliverance God repeatedly offered the Hebrews throughout their cycles of rebellion in Judges. Remember David's gracious treatment of his adversary Saul, even when he had a golden opportunity for revenge in 1 Samuel 26. Add to that David's bounteous grace in dealing with Mephibosheth, Saul's relative in 2 Samuel 9. And then there is God's gracious deliverance of the recalcitrant prophet Jonah from drowning in Jonah 1:17 and 2:10. Not to mention the grace He showed in the face of the prophet's anger in chapter 4.

In the New Testament

Gather almost any handful of verses in the New Testament, take a deep whiff, and you'll find them redolent with grace. Look at Matthew 9:10–12, for example.

> And it happened that as He was reclining at the table in the house, behold many tax-gatherers and sinners came and were dining with Jesus and His disciples. And when the Pharisees saw this, they said to His disciples, "Why is your Teacher eating with the tax-gatherers and sinners?" But when He heard this, He said, "It is not those who are healthy who need a physician, but those who are sick."

The seed that Jesus planted in His disciples' minds in Matthew 9 finally took root in Peter's life in Acts 10:28.

> And he said to them, "You yourselves know how unlawful it is for a man who is a Jew to associate with a foreigner or to visit him; and yet God has shown me that I should not call any man unholy or unclean."[4]

4. See also verses 9–16.

Just like the stuffed-shirted, straight-laced Pharisees in Jesus' time, there will always be people who do not want you to enjoy the liberty of God's grace. They will attempt to pour you into their mold. If you refuse, they'll criticize you. Watch out for them. Their favorite method is to intimidate you. Their favorite response is to get you to imitate them. Their favorite objective is to destroy your freedom by bringing you into subjection.

Some Practical Expectations

Living by grace is our only defense against legalism. And here are four things you can expect if you live according to the "grace principle." First, you will have a greater appreciation of the gifts God has given you. Second, you will spend less time and energy preoccupied with other people's choices. Third, you will become more tolerant and joyful while becoming less prejudiced and judgmental. Fourth, you will take a giant step toward maturity.

Live by grace and, before you know it, your face will begin to show it. Live by legalism and your face will eventually show its effects too. The real question you have to ask yourself is this: Do I want to look like a Pharisee or do I want to look like Jesus?

 Living Insights STUDY ONE

Meditate on the following words by the renowned British theologian Malcolm Muggeridge.

> In the face of a Mother Teresa I trace the very geography of Jesus's Kingdom; all the contours and valleys and waterways. I need no other map. . . .
>
> . . . In the dismal slums of Calcutta a Mother Teresa and her Missionaries of Charity go about Jesus's work of love with incomparable dedication. When I think of them, as I have seen them at their work and at their devotions, I want to put away all the books, tear up all the scribbled notes. There are no more doubts or dilemmas; everything is perfectly clear. What commentary or exposition, however eloquent, lucid, perceptive, inspired even, can equal in elucidation and illumination the effect of these dedicated lives? What mind has conceived a discourse, or tongue

spoken it, which conveys even to a minute degree the light they shine before men? *I was an hungred, and ye gave me meat; I was thirsty, and ye gave me drink: I was a stranger, and ye took me in: naked and ye clothed me: I was sick, and ye visited me: I was in prison, and ye came unto me*—the words come alive, as no study or meditation could possibly make them, in the fulfilment in the most literal sense of Jesus's behest to see in the suffering face of humanity his suffering face, and in their broken bodies, his.[5]

Describe what people see when they look into *your* face.

_____

_____

_____

_____

_____

_____

What do they see of Jesus' face in yours?

_____

_____

_____

_____

_____

 Living Insights

In the windswept harbor of New York City stands a stately lady robed in the verdigris of weathered copper. Her left arm is wrapped around a tablet signifying our Declaration of Independence. Her right arm proudly holds a torch. At her feet lies a broken shackle.

5. Malcolm Muggeridge, *Jesus: The Man Who Lives* (1975; reprint, New York, N.Y.: Harper and Row, Publishers, 1987), pp. 73, 71.

At the base of the august Statue of Liberty is a bronze tablet inscribed with these words:

> Give me your tired, your poor,
> Your huddled masses yearning to breathe free.[6]

Lady Liberty echoes Christ's call to the downtrodden two thousand years earlier:

> "Come to Me, all you who are weary and heavy-laden, and I will give you rest." (Matt. 11:28)

Are you tired of trying to measure up to someone else's rigid rules for living life? Do you yearn to be free from all that? Are you weary from the load some legalistic teacher has placed on your back? Are you ready for a rest?

If so, listen to what the Savior has to say in the two verses that follow Matthew 11:28.

> "Take My yoke upon you, and learn from Me, for I am gentle and humble in heart; and you shall find rest for your souls. For my yoke is easy, and My load is light."

- Is the yoke you're living under one that's been placed there by

  ☐ your parents?   ☐ a Bible teacher?

  ☐ your past?   ☐ Jesus?

  ☐ your church?

- Describe it.

_____

_____

_____

_____

_____

_____

6. Emma Lazarus, "The New Colossus," in _Poems That Live Forever_, comp. Hazel Felleman (New York, N.Y.: Doubleday, 1965), n.p.

- How can you break free from that yoke?

_____

_____

_____

- From Matthew 11:28–30, what are the responsibilities in following Christ?

_____

_____

_____

- What are the rewards?

_____

_____

_____

If legalism has kept you on a short leash with a chafing collar, why not break out of that constricting way of life and learn about grace from the One who was grace incarnate. Remember, He died to set us free, not to enslave us, as Paul affirms so emphatically in Galatians 5:1:

> It was for freedom that Christ set us free; therefore keep standing firm and do not be subject again to a yoke of slavery.

Chapter 2

THE FREE GIFT

Selected Scriptures

Satan's favorite philosophy filters down to humanity and pollutes the way it thinks. This philosophy has become the theme of a plethora of political speeches and the topic of countless commencement addresses. It is rooted in the academic community. It flowers in the furrows of prideful minds. And it reaches fruition in the immaculately manicured gardens of many writers and poets.

One such poet, William Ernest Henley, represents this philosophy in his poem "Invictus."

> Out of the night that covers me,
>   Black as the Pit from pole to pole,
> I thank whatever gods may be
>   For my unconquerable soul.
>
> In the fell clutch of circumstance
>   I have not winced nor cried aloud.
> Under the bludgeonings of chance
>   My head is bloody, but unbowed.
>
> Beyond this place of wrath and tears
>   Looms but the Horror of the shade,
> And yet the menace of the years
>   Finds and shall find me unafraid.
>
> It matters not how strait the gate,
>   How charged with punishments the scroll,
> I am the master of my fate:
>   I am the captain of my soul.[1]

What is this philosophy? The myth of human self-sufficiency, one of the grand illusions of our time . . . and one of the greatest heresies.

---

1. William Ernest Henley, "Invictus," in *The Best Loved Poems of the American People*, comp. Hazel Felleman (Garden City, N.Y.: Garden City Publishing Co., 1936), p. 73.

Warning: Heresy on the Loose

The seed of this enticing heresy was first sown in the Garden of Eden by Satan himself. Beguiled by the promises of the serpent, Adam and Eve took the fruit of the forbidden tree and ate. And the world has been suffering from food poisoning ever since.

What is this heresy of self-sufficiency? It is an emphasis on what *we* do for God instead of what *God* does and has done for us. It may sound harmless, but if you feed on that philosophy very long, it will satiate you with yourself, and you'll become so full you won't feel any hunger for God.

How does this heresy think? Genesis 11 provides an excellent example. In ancient times, before there were languages and dialects and before people were divided into tribes and nations, humanity was one indivisible mass. By unanimous vote, this prodigious union embarked on an equally prodigious building project.

> Now the whole earth used the same language and the same words. And it came about as they journeyed east, that they found a plain in the land of Shinar and settled there. And they said to one another, "Come, let us make bricks and burn them thoroughly." And they used brick for stone, and they used tar for mortar. And they said, "Come let us build for ourselves a city, and a tower whose top will reach into heaven, and let us make for ourselves a name; lest we be scattered abroad over the face of the whole earth." (vv. 1–4)

Note the emphasis on human effort and reputation: "let *us* make bricks and burn them . . . let *us* build for ourselves a city, and a tower . . . let *us* make for ourselves a name."

The Living Bible calls this tower "a proud, eternal monument to themselves." It was to be a tower whose top would reach into heaven (v. 4). The verse literally says, "with its top in the heavens."[2] Somehow the upper part of this tower would be associated with the heavens. But what is the meaning of this cryptic description? Archeology may have unearthed the answer.

A number of years ago, extensive diggings were conducted in the

---

2. U. Cassuto, *A Commentary on the Book of Genesis*, pt. 2, *From Noah to Abraham*, trans. Israel Abrahams (Jerusalem, Israel: The Magnes Press, The Hebrew University, 1964), p. 242.

region of Shinar (v. 2) that uncovered several ziggurats—cone-shaped towers with spiral staircases wrapped around them. One of these ziggurats stood out above all the rest. In the uppermost stones were etched signs of the zodiac and astral figures. This mural was a representation of the heavens and formed something of a religious shrine. For those star worshipers, it was a way they could cling to religion without emptying their hands of their works. It was a way they could give nodding assent to a higher deity without having to abdicate the throne of their hearts.

What was the Lord's reaction to this high-handed heresy?

> And the Lord came down to see the city and the tower which the sons of men had built. And the Lord said, "Behold, they are one people, and they all have the same language. And this is what they began to do, and now nothing which they purpose to do will be impossible for them. Come, let Us go down and there confuse their language, that they may not understand one another's speech." So the Lord scattered them abroad from there over the face of the whole earth; and they stopped building the city. Therefore its name was called Babel, because there the Lord confused the language of the whole earth; and from there the Lord scattered them abroad over the face of the whole earth. (vv. 5–9)

Due to the babbling incoherence of the workers, the construction project lurched to a halt. It's interesting, though, that God did not destroy the tower. Instead, He left it as a mute reminder of the futility of that heresy and as a towering indictment against a religion of human works.

Defending: Truth on the Scaffold

To warn of the heresy of human works is not enough. We must also defend the truth that has been dethroned. James Russell Lowell, a contemporary of William Ernest Henley, speaks of dethroned truth in a poem of hope.

> Truth forever on the scaffold, Wrong forever on
> the throne—
> Yet that scaffold sways the future, and, behind
> the dim unknown,

12

Standeth God within the shadow, keeping watch
above his own.[3]

At the heart of defending the truth of God's sufficiency is a
single word, pulsating with life — *grace*.

One of the most compelling examples of grace in the Bible is
Abraham. If ever there was a man who could have pulled himself
up by the bootstraps of his own works, it was Abraham. He was
wealthy, well-respected, and had a wonderful wife. Yet he was still
completely without hope of ever earning God's favor.

Then, out of the clear blue sky, God reached down and sover-
eignly chose him. A choice that was made not on the basis of works
but grace.

> What then shall we say that Abraham, our fore-
> father according to the flesh, has found? For if
> Abraham was justified by works, he has something
> to boast about; but not before God. For what does the
> Scripture say? "And Abraham believed God, and it
> was reckoned to him as righteousness." (Rom. 4:1–3)

God's Work . . . Not Human Effort

What was it that justified Abraham before God? His social
standing? His sincerity? His service? No, none of these even moved
the scale so much as a millimeter, as Donald Barnhouse notes in
his commentary.

> The day came when, in the accounting of God,
> ungodly Abraham was suddenly declared righteous.
> There was nothing in Abraham that caused the action;
> it began in God and went out to the man in sover-
> eign grace. Upon a sinner the righteousness of God
> was placed. In the accounting the very righteousness
> of God was reckoned, credited, and imputed. The
> Lord God Himself, by an act of grace moved by His
> sovereign love, stooped to the record and blotted
> out everything that was against Abraham, and then
> wrote down on the record that He, God, counted,
> reckoned, credited, imputed this man Abraham to

---

3. *Bartlett's Familiar Quotations*, 15th ed., rev. and enl., ed. Emily Morison Beck (Boston,
Mass.: Little, Brown and Co., 1980), p. 567.

be perfect even at a moment when Abraham was ungodly in himself. That is justification.[4]

The next two verses in Romans state it even more clearly.

Now to the one who works, his wage is not reckoned as a favor, but as what is due. But to the one who does not work, but believes in Him who justifies the ungodly, his faith is reckoned as righteousness. (vv. 4–5)

Our earthly economy is built on a system of rewards for work rendered. You work, you earn a wage. The harder and longer you work, the more wages you earn. God's economy is built on the opposite premise. Grace is not something you work for. It's not something you earn. It's a gift (Eph. 2:8–9). Consequently, there's no room for boasting, all the credit goes to God.

The thief on the cross is a classic example that God's grace is not based on effort. Not only did the thief do no work, he couldn't have if he tried. All he could do while he was hanging on that cross was believe (Luke 23:39–43).

Free Gift . . . Not Earned Wage

Continuing the discussion of grace in Romans 5:1, Paul leaves the example of Abraham and makes an application to us.

Therefore having been justified by faith, we have peace with God through our Lord Jesus Christ.

The verse affirms that we are justified by faith—not works. The result is that we have "peace with God." The means is "through our Lord Jesus Christ."

And why do we need this "peace with God"? Because Adam's fall was the Pandora's box that released sin into the world, infecting every man, woman, and child.

Therefore, just as through one man sin entered into the world, and death through sin, and so death spread to all men, because all sinned—for until the Law sin was in the world; but sin is not imputed when there is no law. Nevertheless death reigned

---

4. Donald Grey Barnhouse, *God's Remedy; God's River* (1954, 1959; reprint, Grand Rapids, Mich.: William B. Eerdmans Publishing Co., 1973), vol. 2, p. 208.

from Adam until Moses, even over those who had
not sinned in the likeness of the offense of Adam,
who is a type of Him who was to come. (5:12–14)

As a microbiologist isolates and classifies a virus to differentiate
it from healthy cells, so the Law isolates and classifies sin. It shows
sin to be a deadly transgression against God's will. In doing so, the
Law intensifies our guilt and adds insult to our already injured
consciences. Just as a Keep Off the Grass sign increases our desire
to trespass, so the Law stimulates our desire to sin (v. 20a).

But the good news is that there's a cure to this deadly epidemic.

So then as through one transgression there resulted
condemnation to all men, even so through one act
of righteousness there resulted justification of life to
all men. For as through the one man's disobedience
the many were made sinners, even so through the
obedience of the One the many will be made righteous. (vv. 18–19)

The Law was never meant to be a ziggurat of moral steps to
climb our way to heaven. It was meant to be a light to reveal the
sin that cowered in the dusty corners and dark closets of our lives.
But the Law could only reveal. It couldn't rescue.

Seeing us in bondage to our sin and shackled to our selfish ways,
grace came to the rescue. Grace was the key in the hand of God
that unlocked our prison door and set us free.

But where sin increased, grace abounded all the
more, that, as sin reigned in death, even so grace
might reign through righteousness to eternal life
through Jesus Christ our Lord. (vv. 20b–21)

No matter how formidable the stone walls of sin that surround
us, God's grace is more formidable. No matter how stalwart the iron
cells that imprison us, God's grace is more stalwart. No matter how
sure the shackles that bind us, God's grace is surer still.

Explaining: Grace for the Sinful

The final passage we want to look at today is Ephesians 2, which
both diagnoses our condition and dispenses a prescription.

Our Condition

If you embrace a humanistic philosophy of life, Ephesians 2 will come as a bracing affront.

> And you were dead in your trespasses and sins, in which you formerly walked according to the course of this world, according to the prince of the power of the air, of the spirit that is now working in the sons of disobedience. Among them we too all formerly lived in the lusts of our flesh, indulging the desires of the flesh and of the mind, and were by nature children of wrath, even as the rest. (vv. 1–3)

Not a very flattering picture, is it? Skip down to verse 12 and the picture gets even bleaker.

> Remember that you were at that time separate from Christ, excluded from the commonwealth of Israel, and strangers to the covenants of promise, having no hope and without God in the world.

Separated . . . excluded . . . strangers . . . no hope. What a desperate condition. Hardly something you'd find in *The Humanist Manifesto*.

God's Solution

Our condition is bad news, like a doctor telling us we have a terminal disease. But the gospel is good news, and that's found beginning in verse 4.

> But God, being rich in mercy, because of His great love with which He loved us, even when we were dead in our transgressions, made us alive together with Christ (by grace you have been saved), and raised us up with Him, and seated us with Him in the heavenly places, in Christ Jesus, in order that in the ages to come He might show the surpassing riches of His grace in kindness toward us in Christ Jesus. For by grace you have been saved through faith; and that not of yourselves, it is the gift of God; not as a result of works, that no one should boast. (vv. 4–9)

We are not invincible captains of our souls as William Henley says. We cannot strut through the stanzas of "Invictus" with our heads held high. Our salvation is a gift of God, not of works, and we have no room to boast. Instead we should bow our heads in homage to the One who is the true captain of our souls—Jesus Christ.

> Out of the light that dazzles me,
>   Bright as the sun from pole to pole,
> I thank the God I know to be
>   For Christ the conqueror of my soul.
>
> Since His the sway of circumstance,
>   I would not wince nor cry aloud.
> Under that rule which men call chance
>   My head with joy is humbly bowed.
>
> Beyond this place of sin and tears
>   That life with Him! And His the aid,
> Despite the menace of the years,
>   Keeps, and shall keep me, unafraid.
>
> I have no fear, though strait the gate,
>   He cleared from punishment the scroll.
> Christ is the Master of my fate,
>   Christ is the Captain of my soul.[5]

 Living Insights

The cornerstone of the American work ethic is a reliance on our own effort, on pulling ourselves up by our own bootstraps. Our favorite verse is: "God helps those who help themselves."

The only problem is that this verse isn't found in the Bible. It's found in *Poor Richard's Almanac*, written by Benjamin Franklin.[6]

Let's turn to some genuine Bible verses to find out what God has to say about Franklin's creed. As you look up the following passages, summarize what each has to say.

---

5. Dorothea Day, "My Captain," in *Best Loved Poems of the American People*, pp. 73–74.

6. The saying is not original with Franklin but is an echo from one of Aesop's fables, "Hercules and the Wagoner." Further research indicates that Aesop cribbed it from the Greek philosophers. Aeschylus (525–456 B.C.), for example, said: "God loves to help him who strives to help himself." Euripides (485–406 B.C.) voiced a similar philosophy: "Try first thyself, and after call in God; / For to the worker God himself lends aid." See *Bartlett's Familiar Quotations*, pp. 347, 66.

1 Corinthians 1:26–29 _____

_____

Galatians 2:16 _____

_____

2 Timothy 1:9 _____

_____

Now use those passages to articulate a response to Poor Richard's philosophy.

_____

_____

_____

_____

_____

🌹 *Living Insights*

If the grace of God comes to us apart from human effort, does that mean we are justified in becoming "couch-potato" Christians?

- Look up Ephesians 2:8–10, and describe "works" in their proper context.

_____

_____

_____

_____

- What is the purpose of good works (see Matt. 5:14–16)?

_____

_____

- What is the source of our good works (see John 15:1–5; Phil. 2:13)?

  _____

  _____

- What is the motivation for our works (see Matt. 25:14–30; 2 Cor. 5:9–10; Col. 3:23–24)?

  _____

  _____

  _____

  _____

Chapter 3

ISN'T GRACE RISKY?

Selected Scriptures

Sermons about salvation by grace alone often open a can of theological worms that wriggle their way into our minds. *Isn't the gospel of grace risky?* we ask ourselves as we squirm in our pews.

Certainly it is. Martyn Lloyd-Jones, pastor of England's Westminster Chapel for thirty years, noted this risk in his commentary on Romans.

> If it is true that where sin abounded grace has much more abounded, well then, 'shall we continue in sin, that grace may abound yet further?'
>
> First of all let me make a comment, to me a very important and vital comment. The true preaching of the gospel of salvation by grace alone always leads to the possibility of this charge being brought against it. There is no better test as to whether a man is really preaching the New Testament gospel of salvation than this, that some people might misunderstand it and misinterpret it to mean that it really amounts to this, that because you are saved by grace alone it does not matter at all what you do; you can go on sinning as much as you like because it will redound all the more to the glory of grace. That is a very good test of gospel preaching. If my preaching and presentation of the gospel of salvation does not expose it to that misunderstanding, then it is not the gospel.[1]

If a pastor preaches legalism—a message of salvation based on the merits of one's works—no one will ever bring that charge against him. But if he preaches grace—salvation by faith alone— then that is risky homiletical business.

---

1. D. M. Lloyd-Jones, *Romans: An Exposition of Chapter 6, The New Man* (Grand Rapids, Mich.: Zondervan Publishing House, 1972), p. 8.

The Reality of the Risk

In order for anyone to stand before a just and holy God, that person must be righteous. Hence the need for justification.

> Therefore having been justified by faith, we have peace with God through our Lord Jesus Christ. (Rom. 5:1)

Justification is a theological word we often take for granted without taking the time to define. It refers to the sovereign act of God whereby He declares righteous the believing sinner while he or she is still in a state of sin. It doesn't mean that the believing sinner stops sinning or that the believing sinner is *made* righteous, in the sense of being perfected. It means the person is *declared* righteous. It is a judicial pronouncement made on the basis of Christ's righteousness and His substitutionary death on the cross.

To believe by grace and to live by grace include the reality of risk. Most people find this uncomfortable. Most want some moral report card that objectively measures their progress. Works provide that. But if works are not the basis of our relationship with God, then there is no *external* proof of salvation or spirituality. If, on the other hand, grace is the basis of our relationship with God, then the reality of our faith is *internal*. It can be seen—and judged—only by God.

To be sure, there are those who abuse this doctrine, saying they have truly believed when they have not. And some live on the edge, flirting with the world and squandering their spiritual inheritance in prodigal indulgence. But abuse is part of the risk that grace has chosen to take.

The fear of its abuse is what causes many ministers to refrain from emphasizing grace. As a result, they emphasize works, provide performance lists for people to live up to, leave no room for gray areas, and cultivate judgmental attitudes toward those who may not agree with them.

Such constricting yokes are often an attempt to keep their parishioners in line. But the line is not one marked by Scripture. It is a legalistic line drawn more from the personal preferences of the pastor or from the congregation itself.

That is not the yoke the Lord Jesus offers (Matt. 11:28–30). He said, "You shall know the truth, and the truth shall make you free. . . . If therefore the Son shall make you free, you shall be free indeed" (John 8:32, 36).

All of this newfound freedom comes to us by grace. God gives us grace to believe—a faith that is not deserved; and He gives us grace to live—a lifestyle that is not dictated.

The Inescapable Tension

Because of grace we have been freed from sin's slavery, from bondage to sinful attitudes, urges, and actions. But that creates a tension. Once we become free in Christ and live by grace, we can take our liberty to an extreme and live a life of license. Paul addresses this tension in Romans 6:1–15.

> What shall we say then? Are we to continue in sin that grace might increase? May it never be! How shall we who died to sin still live in it? Or do you not know that all of us who have been baptized into Christ Jesus have been baptized into His death? Therefore we have been buried with Him through baptism into death, in order that as Christ was raised from the dead through the glory of the Father, so we too might walk in newness of life. For if we have become united with Him in the likeness of His death, certainly we shall be also in the likeness of His resurrection, knowing this, that our old self was crucified with Him, that our body of sin might be done away with, that we should no longer be slaves to sin; for he who has died is freed from sin. Now if we have died with Christ, we believe that we shall also live with Him, knowing that Christ, having been raised from the dead, is never to die again; death no longer is master over Him. For the death that He died, He died to sin, once for all; but the life that He lives, He lives to God. Even so consider yourselves to be dead to sin, but alive to God in Christ Jesus.
>
> Therefore do not let sin reign in your mortal body that you should obey its lusts, and do not go on presenting the members of your body to sin as instruments of unrighteousness; but present yourselves to God as those alive from the dead, and your members as instruments of righteousness to God. For sin shall not be master over you, for you are not under law, but under grace.

> What then? Shall we sin because we are not
> under law but under grace? May it never be!

The freedom we have in Christ is not a freedom to do anything we want to do, but to be everything God created us to be. Before our conversion we were enslaved to sin. Since then, we've become emancipated—not to run riot through the dead-end alleyways of self-indulgence, but to serve a greater master . . . righteousness (see v. 18).

Maybe an illustration would help bring the concept down to earth. Suppose you were given the keys to a new car whose speedometer went to 120 mph. Does it follow that you have the right to race through the streets with reckless abandon? To go on a joyride that jeopardizes the safety of everyone you go speeding past? No, certainly not. That's why Paul warned the Galatians to steer their freedom in another direction.

> For you were called to freedom, brethren; only
> do not turn your freedom into an opportunity for the
> flesh, but through love serve one another. (Gal. 5:13)

Joyous Benefits of Being Liberated

With our freedom in Christ come several exciting benefits. We are no longer bound by our fleeting impulses or our flaming desires. We are free to make good, objective choices. We are able to think independently without the tyranny of needing to compare ourselves with others. And we are able to grow toward greater flexibility and maturity into the person God created us to be.

Telltale Signs of Being Irresponsible

Freedom—whether we're talking about it in the political realm or in the moral realm—doesn't imply freedom from responsibility. Some Christians, however, have interpreted their freedom in Christ to be absolute, without restraint and without responsibility to others.

These libertarians are easy to spot. They have a lack of love and concern for others. They rationalize sin. They are unwilling to be accountable. They resist anyone getting close enough to give them advice. And they disregard new converts and those weak in the faith.

Essential Necessity of Balance

Romans 14 talks a lot about responsibility to those with a weaker faith. It also has a lot to say about balance. The important thing is not to adopt someone else's convictions, but to work out your own convictions (see vv. 1–5, 13–14, 19, 22–23).

How do you do this? Picture grace as a tightrope. It's risky stepping out. Understandably, you're afraid. Especially since there are very few hard-and-fast rules to follow. Really, there are only two. The first is to get over the fear of heights, of walking without the safety of well-traveled ground underneath you. The second is to maintain your balance.

God wants you to be sensitive to other people's convictions, but He doesn't want you to be blown off the high wire by the strong winds of other people's opinions. Balance is the only way to survive. And to maintain balance, you have to have a strong center of gravity. To keep that center of gravity in place, you constantly need to think about your life in light of these questions:

> Is this *my* conviction before God (Rom. 14:22a)?
> Do I have an inner peace and pleasure in it (v. 22b)?
> Am I free of doubt (v. 23)?

Practical Suggestions for Guarding against Extremes

Legalism and license lie on opposite extremes. In the middle is love—love for God and love for other people. To live your life in that middle ground of grace, you need balance. Here are three suggestions to help you strike that balance in your life.

First: *Enjoy the freedom grace provides.* You may have difficulty at first stepping beyond the No Trespassing signs some legalists have put in your way. But there's no reason to feel guilty or afraid. Simply give yourself the permission to be free, to walk without the fear of someone looking over your shoulder (compare Gal. 2:4).

Second: *Treat grace as an undeserved privilege rather than an exclusive right.* Live gratefully, not arrogantly. Have fun, but don't flaunt it. It's all in the attitude, really. It has little to do with what we buy or how we dress or what movies we allow ourselves to see.

Third: *Remember that while grace came to you freely, it cost the Savior His life.* There was no cheap grace that flowed from the veins of Christ on the cross. Each drop was of incalculable value to the Father. And if you so value that gift, you will never have to worry about abusing grace. Remember, He died that you might live . . . and that you might live free.

Broadcast Schedule

The Grace Awakening

September 3–October 22, 1996

Tuesday	September 3	**The Grace Awakening: A 1996 Introduction*** Selected Scriptures
Wednesday	September 4	**The Grace Awakening: A 1996 Introduction***
Thursday	September 5	**Grace: It's *Really* Amazing** Selected Scriptures
Friday	September 6	**Grace: It's *Really* Amazing**
Monday	September 9	**The Free Gift** Selected Scriptures
Tuesday	September 10	**The Free Gift**
Wednesday	September 11	**The Free Gift**
Thursday	September 12	**Isn't Grace Risky?** Selected Scriptures
Friday	September 13	**Isn't Grace Risky?**
Monday	September 16	**Undeserving, Yet Unconditionally Loved** 1 Corinthians 15:9–11; 2 Samuel 9
Tuesday	September 17	**Undeserving, Yet Unconditionally Loved**
Wednesday	September 18	**Squaring Off Against Legalism** Selected Scriptures from Galatians
Thursday	September 19	**Squaring Off Against Legalism**
Friday	September 20	**Emancipated? Then Live Like It!** Romans 6:1–14; 1 John 1:9
Monday	September 23	**Emancipated? Then Live Like It!**
Tuesday	September 24	**Guiding Others to Freedom** Romans 6:15–23 and Selected Scriptures
Wednesday	September 25	**Guiding Others to Freedom**
Thursday	September 26	**Guiding Others to Freedom**
Friday	September 27	**The Grace to Let Others Be** Romans 14

Monday	September 30	The Grace to Let Others Be
Tuesday	October 1	Graciously Disagreeing and Pressing On Acts 15:36–41; Ephesians 4:29–32
Wednesday	October 2	Graciously Disagreeing and Pressing On
Thursday	October 3	Grace: Up Close and Personal Selected Scriptures
Friday	October 4	Grace: Up Close and Personal

Monday	October 7	Are You Really a Minister of Grace? Selected Scriptures
Tuesday	October 8	Are You Really a Minister of Grace?
Wednesday	October 9	Are You Really a Minister of Grace?
Thursday	October 10	A Marriage Oiled by Grace Selected Scriptures
Friday	October 11	A Marriage Oiled by Grace

Monday	October 14	The Charming Joy of Grace Giving 2 Corinthians 9:3–8, 13–14; 2 Corinthians 8:1–9
Tuesday	October 15	The Charming Joy of Grace Giving
Wednesday	October 16	Grace: It's *Really* Accepting Selected Scriptures
Thursday	October 17	Grace: It's *Really* Accepting
Friday	October 18	Grace: It's *Really* Accepting

Monday	October 21	The Grace Awakening: A 1996 Epilogue* Selected Scriptures
Tuesday	October 22	The Grace Awakening: A 1996 Epilogue*

* New messages especially prepared for this rebroadcast.

Broadcast schedule subject to change without notice

Insight for Living • Post Office Box 69000, Anaheim, CA 92817-0900
Insight for Living Ministries • Post Office Box 2510, Vancouver, BC, Canada V6B 3W7
Insight for Living, Inc. • GPO Box 2823 EE, Melbourne, VIC 3001, Australia

Printed in the United States of America

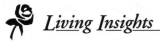

Living by grace is risky. At first the tightrope looks like a thin thread stretched in front of you. You look down, and the height makes you light-headed. You step out on that rope, and your legs wobble like a newborn colt, with gusts of wind making you teeter.

How do you conquer that fear of walking by grace? You conquer it one step at a time. Practice, won't you, on the tightrope that runs through Romans 14.

- What two controversial issues are addressed in the passage?

  1. _____

  2. _____

- Can different convictions be equally acceptable before God? Support your answer from verses in the passage.

  _____

  _____

  _____

- What is important to God about your convictions?

  _____

  _____

- How should the more mature believer respond to the believer who is still struggling to get a firm footing in the faith?

  _____

- What danger does the stronger believer face in focusing on the weaker believer's opinions?

  _____

- What danger does the weaker believer face in focusing on the stronger believer's opinions?

  _____

- What should the guiding principle be in your relationship with all believers, even if their convictions are diametrically opposed to yours?

  _____

  _____

- Why is passing judgment on another person's opinions presumptuous?

  _____

  _____

- List some gray-area issues that might be mentioned in Romans 14 if the letter were written today.

  _____

  _____

  _____

  _____

  _____

  _____

- Which of those issues causes the most controversy between you and other believers?

  _____

- In light of Romans 14, what adjustments should you make in your attitude toward other believers who stand on the opposite side of the fence?

  _____

  _____

  _____

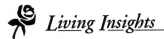

People come up with lists for a number of reasons. Sometimes a list is merely for organizational purposes. Sometimes it's to keep us from harm, like the list of precautions on a bottle of medicine. Sometimes, however, the list is written as a kind of yardstick that we're required to stand under so that others can measure our spiritual progress. This list of "Thou shalts" and "Thou shalt nots" may be written, spoken, or simply communicated with a raised eyebrow. But whatever form the list takes, it's legalism—and it's lethal to your spiritual life.

Let's take a few minutes to reflect on any legalistic lists that may have controlled your life in the past. Write down the lists of binding but nonbiblical constraints that you were forced to conform to as you were growing up.

From Your Parents

_____

_____

_____

_____

_____

From Your Peer Group

_____

_____

_____

_____

From Your Church

_____

_____

_____

_____

From Your School

_____

_____

_____

_____

From Yourself

_____

_____

_____

_____

Of those you wrote down, which ones still follow you around and wag a finger when you don't measure up?

_____

_____

_____

_____

Which one most limits your freedom in Christ and keeps you from growing in grace?

_____

Take a moment now to listen to Christ carefully and prayerfully, asking Him what you need to do to free yourself from that chafing wooden yoke of legalism. Write down any liberating thoughts He may bring to mind.

_____

_____

_____

_____

Chapter 4

UNDESERVING, YET UNCONDITIONALLY LOVED

1 Corinthians 15:9–11; 2 Samuel 9

To many people, grace is little more than something said before
dinner. To others, the word is applied to a coordinated gym-
nast who moves through the air with fluid ease. Sometimes it's used
as a verb to describe the presence of nobility at a gathering: "The
queen graced the meeting with her presence." Other times it refers
to a genteel quality. And at still other times it's used as a name for
a baby girl. All of these usages, however, pale by comparison to the
richness and splendor of the word as it's used in Scripture.

Biblically, *grace* means "unmerited favor." It is our only hope as
sinful human beings. And it is the method we are to use when
relating to others.

Listen to the words of the apostle Paul as he described the very
transformation of his life brought about by God's grace.

> For I am the least of the apostles, who am not fit to
> be called an apostle, because I persecuted the church
> of God. But by the grace of God I am what I am,
> and His grace toward me did not prove vain; but I
> labored even more than all of them, yet not I, but
> the grace of God with me. (1 Cor. 15:9–10)

Grace transformed Paul from an archenemy of the Christian
faith to its staunchest defender; from a rigid, legalistic Pharisee to
a compassionate, Christlike person. God's grace can do the same
for us. There is no heart so hard that His grace cannot soften it,
no life so low that His grace cannot lift it to exalted heights.

Reaffirming the Truth of Grace

If we were to sum up Paul's credo on grace, we could do so in
three single-syllable statements:

1. God does what He does by grace.
2. I am what I am by the grace of God.
3. I let you be what you are by the grace of God.

Isn't that generous? Who couldn't flourish in soil like that?

We, however, unlike our Lord, prefer to give people what we think they deserve rather than going beyond that and giving what may be undeserved. We like the sermon from Sinai rather than the Sermon on the Mount. We like the idea of "an eye for an eye, and a tooth for a tooth" rather than turning the other cheek (Matt. 5:38–39). And we like performing moral makeovers on people, which are little more than cosmetic in nature. Take the example cited by Elisabeth Elliot in *The Liberty of Obedience*. She writes about a young man eager to follow Christ. Here are the worldly things he was told to forsake in order to follow Christ.

> "Colored clothes, for one thing. Get rid of every-thing in your wardrobe that is not white. Stop sleep-ing on a soft pillow. Sell your musical instruments and don't eat any more white bread. You cannot, if you are sincere about obeying Christ, take warm baths or shave your beard. To shave is to lie against Him who created us, to attempt to improve on His work."[1]

Sounds absurd, doesn't it? Even comical. But hold onto your hair, lest this blow you away: this was the list given in the most acclaimed Christian schools in the second century!

Before we roll on the floor howling with laughter, what do you think our own list of legalistic rules will sound like to those who are a few generations in the future? What list of do's and don'ts have we concocted? What merit badges must others earn to be accepted into our circle of conditional love? A more trenchant question: Who gave us the right to give to someone else the rules to live by?

We need a grace awakening, don't we?

For there to be genuine growth, people must be given space, even room to fail. If they are to ever walk by grace, they must be allowed the freedom to fall on their faces. For it is in stumbling that we learn to walk safely. Grace must be risked, or we'll produce Christians with stunted growth who can't think for themselves and who are forced to live under the tyranny of another's expectations and demands.

---

1. Quoted by Jackie Hudson in *Doubt: A Road to Growth* (San Bernardino, Calif.: Here's Life Publishers, 1987), p. 105.

Considering an Example of Grace

It's one thing to talk about grace; it's another thing to see it enfleshed in a person's life. One of the greatest examples of grace can be seen in the Old Testament in the kindness that David showed to Jonathan's son, Mephibosheth.

In a brutal era when deposed monarchs and their families were exterminated, David would soon be given the throne of King Saul. In what was to be their final battle with the Philistines, both Saul and his son Jonathan were killed. This grieved David greatly, since Jonathan was David's closest friend. The chaos that followed in the wake of that battle caused the family of Saul to flee like frightened field mice. This is the tragic account of one of those who fled.

> Now Jonathan, Saul's son, had a son crippled in his feet. He was five years old when the report of Saul and Jonathan came from Jezreel, and his nurse took him up and fled. And it happened that in her hurry to flee, he fell and became lame. And his name was Mephibosheth. (2 Sam. 4:4)

A Question Asked

In 2 Samuel 9 the story continues. Mephibosheth is now an adult, crippled in both feet. David is not only reigning in all the land, but he is reigning in the hearts of the people. His kingdom has been blessed by God, both on the battlefield and in the fields of the nation's farmers. While reflecting on the abundance of God's blessing, he remembers another blessing God has given him—Jonathan.

Nostalgic about his friendship with Jonathan, the king recalls a vow that the two of them made many years ago.

> Then Jonathan said to David, . . . "If it please my father to do you harm, may the Lord do so to Jonathan and more also, if I do not make it known to you and send you away, that you may go in safety. And may the Lord be with you as He has been with my father. And if I am still alive, will you not show me the lovingkindness of the Lord, that I may not die? And you shall not cut off your lovingkindness from my house forever, not even when the Lord cuts off every one of the enemies of David from the face of the earth." So Jonathan made a covenant with

the house of David, saying, "May the Lord require it at the hands of David's enemies." And Jonathan made David vow again because of his love for him, because he loved him as he loved his own life. (1 Sam. 20:12–17)

That memory flashes across David's mind, prompting him to ask:

"Is there yet anyone left of the house of Saul, that I may show him kindness for Jonathan's sake?" (2 Sam. 9:1)

The Hebrew word translated "kindness" is *chesed*. In the Old Testament it's often rendered as "mercy," "lovingkindness," or "grace." Basking in the kindness that God has shown him, David is moved to pass along the undeserved favor. When he looks around for a beneficiary of that kindness, he doesn't look for someone who is deserving, qualified, or worthwhile. He looks for *anyone* in Saul's house.

Now there was a servant of the house of Saul whose name was Ziba, and they called him to David; and the king said to him, "Are you Ziba?" And he said, "I am your servant." And the king said, "Is there not yet anyone of the house of Saul to whom I may show the kindness of God?" And Ziba said to the king, "There is still a son of Jonathan who is crippled in both feet." So the king said to him, "Where is he?" And Ziba said to the king, "Behold, he is in the house of Machir the son of Ammiel in Lo-debar." (vv. 2–4, emphasis added)

The word *Lo-debar* comes from two Hebrew words, *lo*, which means "no," and *debar*, which means "pasture." It refers to a barren, desolate place, a wasteland.

A Cripple Sought

This wasteland was the last place Mephibosheth ever thought he would hear from a king. But one fine day David's royal summons shows up at his doorstep.

Then King David sent and brought him from the house of Machir the son of Ammiel, from Lo-debar. And Mephibosheth, the son of Jonathan the son of Saul, came to David and fell on his face and prostrated himself. And David said, "Mephibosheth." And he said, "Here is your servant!" (vv. 5–6)

This helpless cripple fell on his face in the trembling awareness that all descendants of previous dynasties were customarily exterminated. He most surely thought that he would never get up from that floor alive.

A Privilege Provided

The words that reach Mephibosheth's ears are not ones of judgment but of mercy. David had not come to kill but to be kind.

> And David said to him, "Do not fear, for I will surely show kindness to you for the sake of your father Jonathan, and will restore to you all the land of your grandfather Saul; and you shall eat at my table regularly." (v. 7)

Notice that there's no mention of individual merit on Mephibosheth's part that he should deserve such kindness. Then it wouldn't be grace. Grace is acceptance without reservation, forgiveness without condemnation, pardon without probation. It is unconditional, unrestrained love.

The result of this outpouring of grace? Check out verses 8–13.

> Again he prostrated himself and said, "What is your servant, that you should regard a dead dog like me?"
> Then the king called Saul's servant Ziba, and said to him, "All that belonged to Saul and to all his house I have given to your master's grandson. And you and your sons and your servants shall cultivate the land for him, and you shall bring in the produce so that your master's grandson may have food; nevertheless Mephibosheth your master's grandson shall eat at my table regularly." Now Ziba had fifteen sons and twenty servants. Then Ziba said to the king, "According to all that my lord the king commands his servant so your servant will do." So Mephibosheth ate at David's table as one of the king's sons. And Mephibosheth had a young son whose name was Mica. And all who lived in the house of Ziba were servants to Mephibosheth. So

Mephibosheth lived in Jerusalem, for he ate at the king's table regularly. Now he was lame in both feet.

Initially, Mephibosheth recoils from the generosity of the king, thinking himself too worthless a creature to receive such favor. But David lifts the crippled man from his prostrate position and seats him at the royal table, a table of uninterrupted provisions and continual nourishment.

Imagine the seating arrangements years from then. The dinner bell would ring and in would come the king to sit at the head of the table. Seated to his left was Amnon . . . next to him, the lovely and gracious Tamar . . . across from them Solomon, intelligent and inquisitive . . . Absalom with his flowing black hair cascading down his shoulders . . . the muscular, bronzed Joab, commander of the troops . . . then hobbling in on a pair of crutches is Mephibosheth, clump, clump, clump.

Amazing grace, how sweet the sound . . . and nobody knew that sound better than Mephibosheth.

Seeing the Analogies of Grace

There are at least eight analogies between the grace that David showed to Mephibosheth and the grace that God has extended to us.

1. Once Mephibosheth had enjoyed fellowship with his father, and so had humanity in the Garden of Eden.

2. When disaster struck, fear came, and Mephibosheth suffered a fall that crippled him for the rest of his life. Similarly, when sin came, humanity suffered a fall, which has left us permanently crippled.

3. Out of unconditional love for his friend Jonathan, David sought out anyone to whom he might extend his grace. In a similar manner, God, because of His unconditional love for His Son and acceptance of His Son's death on the cross, continues to seek anyone to whom He might extend His grace.

4. The crippled man was destitute and undeserving. All he could do was accept the king's favor. So, also, we sinners are undeserving and without hope. In no way are we worthy of our King's favor. All we can do is humbly accept it.

5. The king took the crippled Mephibosheth from a barren wasteland and seated him at the royal banquet table in the palace.

God, our Father, has done the same for us. He rescued us from our own personal Lo-debar, from a moral wasteland, and He seated us in a place of spiritual nourishment and intimacy.

6. David adopted Mephibosheth into his royal family, providing him with every blessing within the palace. We also have been adopted into a family—God's family. And He gives us full privileges within His household.

7. Mephibosheth's limp was a constant reminder of David's grace. So also, our moral feebleness keeps us from ever forgetting that where sin abounds, grace abounds that much more.

8. When Mephibosheth sat at the king's table, he was treated with the same respect and given the same privileges as David's own sons. And when we one day attend the great wedding feast of the Lamb, the same will be true for us as well. We will sit with prophets and priests, apostles and evangelists, pastors and missionaries. We will dine with everyone from Peter to Corrie ten Boom. And we will be there with them because that same tablecloth of grace covers all our feet.

When we, as cripples, sit at that royal banquet table in heaven, we will have so much to be thankful for. And all our praise will go to the Lord Jesus, who is grace incarnate.

> Thou Son of the Blessed! what grace was manifest in thy condescension! Grace brought thee down from heaven; grace stripped thee of thy glory; grace made thee poor and despicable; grace made thee bear such burdens of sin, such burdens of sorrow, such burdens of God's curse, as are unspeakable! O Son of God! grace was in all thy tears! grace came bubbling out of thy side with thy blood! grace came forth with every word of thy sweet mouth! . . . grace came out where the whip smote thee, where the thorn pricked thee, where the nails and spear pierced thee! O blessed Son of God! here is grace indeed! unsearchable riches of grace! unthought of riches of grace! grace to make angels wonder, grace to make sinners happy, grace to astonish devils![2]

2. John Bunyan, *Saved by Grace* (Philadelphia, Pa.: American Baptist Publication Society, 1852), p. 33.

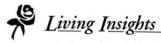

The whole idea of legalistic lists sounds silly when we read them out loud:

- Give up colored clothes.

- Give up sleeping on a soft pillow.

- Give up taking warm baths.

Yet just such stringent standards form the increments on the yardstick that many people use to measure their commitment to Christ. If those standards had been acceptable to God, the Pharisees would have been spiritual giants. But it is not what we give *up* for Christ that matters; it is what we give. And what we are to give is our hearts—completely and passionately.

Look up Luke 7:36–50. Contrast the Pharisee with the repentant woman.

Pharisee	Repentant Woman
_____	_____
_____	_____
_____	_____
_____	_____
_____	_____

Which person was the most respected in the community?

_____

Which one was most revered by Christ? Why?

_____

Describe the relationship between love and forgiveness.

_____

_____

_____

36

From James 4:6, why is grace shown to the repentant woman but not the Pharisee?

_____

_____

For another example similar to the one of the Pharisee and the repentant woman, see Luke 18:9–14. Which of the two people was a legalist?

_____

Which one gained the approval of God?

_____

Which one best describes your life?

_____

🌹 *Living Insights* STUDY TWO

Describe an incident in your past where someone showed you undeserved kindness.

_____

_____

_____

_____

_____

_____

How did it affect your feelings toward that person?

_____

_____

_____

Now describe an incident in your past where someone judged you harshly by a rigid set of legalistic standards.

_____

_____

_____

_____

How did it affect your feelings toward that person?

_____

_____

Has there been a time when God showered you with kindness the way David did Mephibosheth? Describe it.

_____

_____

_____

_____

If so, how did that act of kindness affect your relationship with God?

_____

_____

To conclude your study, meditate on a few passages of Scripture that highlight God's kindness: Psalms 103 and 136; Romans 2:4.

Chapter 5

SQUARING OFF
AGAINST LEGALISM
Selected Scriptures from Galatians

Liberty is worth fighting for. Just ask Patrick Henry, whose fiery rhetoric ignited the Virginia Convention on March 23, 1775, and inflamed the American Revolution.

> If we wish to be free . . . we must fight! I repeat it, sir, we must fight! An appeal to arms, and to the God of hosts, is all that is left us. . . .
>   . . . It is vain, sir, to extenuate the matter. The gentlemen may cry, Peace, peace! but there is no peace. The war has actually begun! . . . Our brethren are already in the field! Why stand we here idle? . . . Is life so dear or peace so sweet as to be purchased at the price of chains and slavery? Forbid it, Almighty God. I know not what course others may take, but as for me, give me liberty or give me death![1]

Ninety years later the fight for liberty continued as the United States found its swords drawn in a civil war over the issue of slavery. On November 5, 1864, Charles Sumner drew the battle lines between the two warring sides.

> Where Slavery is, there Liberty cannot be; and where Liberty is, there Slavery cannot be.[2]

What is so clear with regard to our country, however, is not always so clear with regard to our Christianity. S. Lewis Johnson, Jr., helps bring the threat to our faith's freedom into focus.

> One of the most serious problems facing the orthodox Christian church today is the problem of legalism. One of the most serious problems facing the church in Paul's day was the problem of legalism.

---

1. *Bartlett's Familiar Quotations*, 15th ed., rev. and enl., ed. Emily Morison Beck (Boston, Mass.: Little, Brown and Co., 1980), p. 383.

2. *Bartlett's Familiar Quotations*, p. 539.

In every day it is the same. Legalism wrenches the joy of the Lord from the Christian believer, and with the joy of the Lord goes his power for vital worship and vibrant service. Nothing is left but cramped, somber, dull and listless profession. The truth is betrayed, and the glorious name of the Lord becomes a synonym for a gloomy kill-joy. The Christian under law is a miserable parody of the real thing.[3]

If that last sentence describes you, it's time to square off against legalism. Because if you want to be free, you're gonna have to fight!

Defining Two Significant Terms

So that the distinction between liberty and legalism won't get blurred, let's sharpen the focus even further by defining terms.

Liberty

Liberty is freedom—freedom from sin's slavery to enjoy the abundant life made possible by Christ's sacrifice. It is freedom from the bondage of sin's power and guilt and from God's wrath. It is liberation from the curse of the Law and its relentless demands. It is emancipation from the fear of condemnation and an accusing conscience.

This freedom allows us to revel in Christ's finished work on Calvary and empowers us to become all He means us to be, regardless of how He leads others.

Legalism

Legalism is an attitude that is lawlike in nature. It is an obsessive conformity to a standard for the purpose of exalting self. It is an effective motivator because it uses guilt, which leads to a negative emphasis on what we should *not* be and things we should *not* do.

It is incomprehensible that people who have tasted the fresh water of liberty would ever want to return to the stagnant pools of legalism. But they do. They defect from liberty because the heresy of legalism is so enticing, promising to quench their thirst for acceptance from their peers. But the promise is like an ocean of salt water to a parched tongue. Paul chastised those in Galatia who had lowered their cups into legalism's saline waters.

---

3. S. Lewis Johnson, Jr., "The Paralysis of Legalism," *Bibliotheca Sacra*, April–June 1963, p. 109.

You were running well; who hindered you from obeying the truth? . . .

You foolish Galatians, who has bewitched you, before whose eyes Jesus Christ was publicly portrayed as crucified? . . .

I am amazed that you are so quickly deserting Him who called you by the grace of Christ, for a different gospel. (Gal. 5:7; 3:1; 1:6)

Identifying Three Subtle Adversaries

As we dip into the book of Galatians to sample what's said, a sharp taste grates over our tongues. Paul dilutes no words when it comes to legalism. He comes on strong and straightforward.

In the first two chapters of the book, three adversaries rear their ugly heads. The first is a doctrinal heresy. The second, ecclesiastical harassment. And the third is personal hypocrisy.

Those Who Disturb and Distort through Heresy

Paul wastes no time getting at the heart of the heresy. After five verses of introduction, he rolls up his sleeves and gets right to work.

I am amazed that you are so quickly deserting Him who called you by the grace of Christ, for a different gospel; which is really not another; only there are some who are disturbing you, and want to distort the gospel of Christ. But even though we, or an angel from heaven, should preach to you a gospel contrary to that which we have preached to you, let him be accursed. As we have said before, so I say again now, if any man is preaching to you a gospel contrary to that which you received, let him be accursed. For am I now seeking the favor of men, or of God? Or am I striving to please men? If I were still trying to please men, I would not be a bondservant of Christ. (1:6–10)

The heretical message of the legalists was that the Galatians must let Moses finish what Christ had begun. Theirs was a theology rooted in the Law rather than grace. It appealed to human works, not to the finished work of Christ on the cross.

The good news of the Cross is that salvation begins with the gracious love of God, is carried out by the death and resurrection of His Son, is effected by the Holy Spirit. The results add up to praise for God. But whenever human works is factored into that equation, it distorts the truth. Why? Because it steals some of the glory that rightfully belongs only to God.

Paul felt so strongly about preserving the purity of the gospel that he thought anyone tampering with this pristine truth should be accursed.[4]

These accursed legalists prey on the weak and the compliant, on people pleasers who let themselves be victimized by guilt games that are played against them. The only way to gain victory over those games is to seek to please God alone and to stop striving to please people—to become invincible within and unintimidated without.

Those Who Spy and Enslave through Harassment

As we wade into the second chapter of Galatians, the swamp of legalism grows deeper and thicker, threatening to suck us under into the morass.

> Then after an interval of fourteen years I went up again to Jerusalem with Barnabas, taking Titus along also. And it was because of a revelation that I went up; and I submitted to them the gospel which I preach among the Gentiles, but I did so in private to those who were of reputation, for fear that I might be running, or had run, in vain. But not even Titus who was with me, though he was a Greek, was compelled to be circumcised. But it was because of the false brethren who had sneaked in to spy out our liberty which we have in Christ Jesus, in order to bring us into bondage. But we did not yield in subjection to them for even an hour, so that the truth of the gospel might remain with you. But from those who were of high reputation (what they were makes

---

4. "The Greek word twice translated 'accursed' is *anathema*. It was used in the Greek Old Testament for the divine ban, the curse of God resting upon anything or anyone devoted by Him to destruction. The story of Achan provides an example of this. God said that the spoil of the Canaanites was under His ban—it was devoted to destruction. But Achan stole and kept for himself what should have been destroyed.

So the apostle Paul desires that these false teachers should come under the divine ban, curse or *anathema*. That is, he expresses the wish that God's judgment will fall upon them." John R. W. Stott, *The Message of Galatians* (Downers Grove, Ill.: InterVarsity Press, 1968), p. 24.

no difference to me; God shows no partiality)—well, those who were of reputation contributed nothing to me. (2:1–6)

Some background material will help illuminate the conflict in the above verses.

In the decade or so surrounding the year A.D. 50, the infant church was drifting by degrees and at times almost unnoticeably toward its first great doctrinal crisis. When the gospel was being preached primarily to Jews by Jews, the development of the church progressed smoothly. But as the ambassadors of Christ pushed out into largely Gentile communities and the gospel began to take root there, questions arose regarding a Christian's relationship to the law of Moses and to Judaism as a system. . . .

. . . Was it necessary for a Gentile believer to observe the law of Moses in order to become a Christian? Should a Gentile be circumcised? Questions like these must have been raised with increasing force throughout the Roman Empire, wherever the church of Jesus Christ camped on Gentile soil.[5]

Galatians 2 is a record of a summit meeting that occurred in the early history of the church. Paul went to this gathering with two of his colleagues. One was Barnabas, a circumcised Jew, who was well known and respected. The other was Titus, an uncircumcised Gentile, who was unknown.

The legalists had prompted the meeting, after carrying out their own covert investigation.[6]

That same form of creeping legalism is at work today, surreptitiously pervading every corner of the sanctuary so that not even a church mouse is safe from its suffocating effects. Eugene Peterson writes:

There are people who do not want us to be free. They don't want us to be free before God, accepted

5. James Montgomery Boice, "Galatians," in *The Expositor's Bible Commentary*, ed. Frank E. Gaebelein (Grand Rapids, Mich.: Zondervan Publishing House, Regency Reference Library, 1976), vol. 10, p. 409.

6. The Greek word *kataskopos* means to "spy, to reconnoitre, to make a treacherous investigation." Archibald Thomas Robertson, *Word Pictures in the New Testament* (Nashville, Tenn.: Broadman Press, 1931), vol. 4, p. 284.

just as we are by his grace. They don't want us to be free to express our faith originally and creatively in the world. They want to control us; they want to use us for their own purposes. They themselves refuse to live arduously and openly in faith, but huddle together with a few others and try to get a sense of approval by insisting that all look alike, talk alike and act alike, thus validating one another's worth. They try to enlarge their numbers only on the condition that new members act and talk and behave the way they do. These people infiltrate communities of faith "to spy out our freedom which we have in Christ Jesus" and not infrequently find ways to control, restrict and reduce the lives of free Christians.[7]

Those Who Lie and Deceive through Hypocrisy

The heresy of legalism that led to the harassment of Gentile believers also revealed the hypocrisy that existed within the very highest echelons of the leadership of the church—Peter himself!

> But when Cephas came to Antioch, I opposed him to his face, because he stood condemned. For prior to the coming of certain men from James, he used to eat with the Gentiles; but when they came, he began to withdraw and hold himself aloof, fearing the party of the circumcision. And the rest of the Jews joined him in hypocrisy, with the result that even Barnabas was carried away by their hypocrisy. But when I saw that they were not straightforward about the truth of the gospel, I said to Cephas in the presence of all, "If you, being a Jew, live like the Gentiles and not like the Jews, how is it that you compel the Gentiles to live like Jews?" (vv. 11–14)

Through a revelation recorded in Acts 10, Peter learned of God's acceptance of Gentiles into the family of God and of the abrogation of Jewish dietary laws. As a result, Peter was in the habit of eating meals with the Gentiles.[8] But when a group of rigid Jewish

---

7. Eugene H. Peterson, *Traveling Light: Reflections on the Free Life* (Downers Grove, Ill.: InterVarsity Press, 1982), p. 67.

8. The imperfect tense of the verb "to eat" in Galatians 2:12 indicates continued action, implying that this was Peter's habit pattern.

brothers arrived at the scene, Peter knuckled under to their overpowering presence and backed off from his associations with Gentile believers. And once Paul saw that the hypocrisy had run rampant through the church, he hit the roof.

Hypocrisy is a treacherous thing—acting like you believe one way with a certain set of people, then acting like you believe another way with another group. Legalists are notorious for their hypocrisy. They lack openness, honesty, and vulnerability. They are not real but speak from behind a mask that hides their true identity.[9]

The best way to confuse children is for parents to rear them in a tight, legalistic context of outward religious duty, faking an inward faith and devotion. Our children deserve better than that, don't they? They deserve parents who aren't two-faced hypocrites. They deserve parents who are real, who don't have to hide behind a mask of pious platitudes and religious ritual.

Specifying Four Strong Defenses

Don't ever forget that you are free and that this freedom is worth fighting for. To relinquish it is to give back hard-fought territory to the enemy—the enemy of legalism.

You don't want to live your life behind a fence of false feelings, do you? You don't want your relationship with Christ to be relegated to a rigid set of religious rules. You don't want the new wine that flows so freely from the Lord to be closed up tight, in some old, cracked wineskins. Certainly you don't. You want to live free. You want to be everything God created you to be—not poured into someone else's plastic mold.

If you're determined to live free, you must be equally determined to dig in and fight for that freedom. Here are four bits of advice to help you shovel out a spot for yourself in the trenches.

First: *Keep standing firm in your freedom.* If the group you're in is giving you grief for not living up to their convictions, get out of the group. It's wrong to subject yourself to a group that doesn't respect your convictions and that violates your conscience.

9. The Greek word for "hypocrite" is *hupocritēs*. It refers to an actor playing a part within a play. "In Greek drama the actors held over their faces oversized masks painted to represent the character they were portraying. In life, the hypocrite is a person who masks his real self while he plays a part for his audience." Lawrence O. Richards, *Expository Dictionary of Bible Words* (Grand Rapids, Mich.: Zondervan Publishing House, Regency Reference Library, 1985), see "hypocrite."

Second: *Stop seeking the favor of everyone.* Seek the favor of God alone rather than looking to other people for approval—no matter how spiritual they may seem.

Third: *Start refusing to submit to bondage.* There is no system of slavery as dictatorial and devastating as legalism, for it enslaves our attitudes as well as our actions. It embalms our feelings for Christ rather than emancipating them.

Fourth: *Continue being straightforward about the truth.* Live honestly. When you fall on your face, admit it. When you drop the ball on some responsibility delegated to you, admit it, shoulder the blame, take your consequences like an adult. And remember, no matter how much egg you get on your face, people will usually let you wipe it off . . . if you're honest about it and don't try to cover it up.

 Living Insights

The letter to the Galatians is to Christians what Lincoln's Emancipation Proclamation was to Civil War slaves. It is an official document that proclaims: "You are free!" (see 5:1).

What the Galatians were freed from was the Old Testament Law, a chafing set of leg irons that impeded their walk with Christ. Look up the following references in Galatians, and summarize what is said about the Law.

2:16 _____

_____

2:21 _____

_____

3:2 _____

_____

3:10 _____

_____

3:12 _____

_____

3:13 _____

_____

3:15–18 _____

_____

3:19 _____

_____

3:21 _____

_____

3:23–25 _____

_____

5:4 _____

_____

5:18 _____

_____

 Living Insights STUDY TWO

It's hard to imagine why people once freed from the constraints of the Law would ever want to go back to such a rigid way of life. The reason for the defection is peer pressure. Even as adults we buckle under the pressure exerted on us by our peers.

Whether buying certain clothes to fit in with a country club or saying certain clichés to fit into a church, we're all subject to living under other people's sets of rules.

Let's look in the mirror for a moment as we try one of Paul's questions to the Galatians on for size: Are you striving to please people or are you seeking to please God (1:10)? That's the issue, isn't it? The bottom line: Who are you *really* living to please?

Look up these passages and answer the following questions.

Matthew 6:1–18. What was the problem the Pharisees had?

_____

What is the key to liberating yourself from that form of bondage?

_____

_____

Reconcile 6:1 with 5:16.

_____

_____

_____

2 Corinthians 5:9–10. As new creatures in Christ, what should our goal be?

_____

_____

Why? _____

_____

Colossians 3:22–23. How can we try to please God in a position where demanding people are constantly looking over our shoulder?

_____

_____

It has been said, "Love God and do what you please." Do you agree or disagree?

_____

Explain your answer. _____

_____

_____

Chapter 6

EMANCIPATED?
THEN LIVE LIKE IT!

Romans 6:1–14; 1 John 1:9

Slavery was one of the main issues over which the swords of the Civil War were drawn. It was a bloody conflict, the bloodiest in United States history. The president of the Union, Abraham Lincoln, said of the war in his second inaugural address in 1865, only weeks before he was assassinated:

> Neither party expected for the war, the magnitude, or the duration, which it has already attained. . . . Each looked for an easier triumph. . . . Both read the same Bible, and pray to the same God; and each invokes His aid against the other.[1]

At that point the gaunt, war-worn president's voice cracked. He regained his composure, saying how strange it was

> that any men should dare to ask a just God's assistance in wringing their bread from the sweat of other men's faces.[2]

On New Year's Day, 1863, the Emancipation Proclamation was publicly stated, but it wasn't until December 18, 1865, that the Thirteenth Amendment to the Constitution was officially adopted, abolishing slavery in the United States.

Though the slaves in the South were legally freed, many continued to live as slaves. Shelby Foote, in his three-volume work on the Civil War, documents this unexpected reaction.

> [Most slaves] could repeat, with equal validity, what an Alabama slave had said in 1864 when asked what he thought of the Great Emancipator whose proclamation went into effect that year. "I don't know nothing bout Abraham Lincoln," he replied, "cep

---

1. Quoted by Carl Sandburg in *Abraham Lincoln: The Prairie Years and the War Years*, one volume edition (New York, N.Y.: Harcourt Brace Jovanovich, Publishers, 1982), p. 664.

2. Quoted by Sandburg in *Abraham Lincoln: The Prairie Years and the War Years*, p. 664.

they say he sot us free. And I don't know nothing bout that neither."[3]

Precious blood was spilled to set those slaves free, yet many of them never left the plantations. Many stayed because they feared that life as freed slaves would be more cruel than life on the plantation. But how tragic not to take the risk in order to live free.

Even more tragic is the precious blood spilled at Calvary to set people free spiritually, while Christians still remain enslaved. And they remain enslaved on a sprawling plantation known as legalism.

Reviewing Some Thoughts on Slavery

In this lesson we want to focus on the emancipation proclamation in Romans 6:1–14. But before we do, let's examine the preamble to that proclamation found in chapter 3, verses 10–20.

As it is written,
"There is none righteous, not even one;
"There is none who understands,
There is none who seeks for God;
All have turned aside, together they have
become useless;
There is none who does good,
There is not even one."
"Their throat is an open grave,
With their tongues they keep deceiving,"
"The poison of asps is under their lips";
"Whose mouth is full of cursing and bitterness";
"Their feet are swift to shed blood,
Destruction and misery are in their paths,
And the path of peace have they not known."
"There is no fear of God before their eyes."
Now we know that whatever the Law says, it speaks to those who are under the Law, that every mouth may be closed, and all the world may become accountable to God; because by the works of the Law no flesh will be justified in His sight; for through the Law comes the knowledge of sin.

3. Shelby Foote, *The Civil War: A Narrative* (New York, N.Y.: Random House, 1974), vol. 3, p. 1045.

The book of Romans holds at least three analogies regarding slavery. The first one is based on the above-quoted passage: *All of us were born in bondage to sin*. Although this first analogy is grim, the second is glorious: A *day came when Christ set us free*. That day of redemption is shouted from the rooftops of verses 21–22.

> But now apart from the Law the righteousness of God has been manifested, being witnessed by the Law and the Prophets, even the righteousness of God through faith in Jesus Christ for all those who believe; for there is no distinction.

"No distinction." Don't those words sound wonderful? Redemption is an impartial gift given freely, regardless of our race, sex, age, color, or national origin (v. 24; see also Gal. 3:28; Col. 3:11). Why? Because we are all in the same sinking ship of sin (Rom. 3:23). Christ saw every one of us manacled to that hull, straining futilely at our oars, while the waters of judgment came rushing in through a hole in the bow. Moved with compassion at our plight, Jesus paid the price for the keys to unlock the leg irons that bound us to destruction.

The third analogy to slavery in Romans is tragic: *Many Christians still live as though they are enslaved*. Though emancipated, some Christians don't live like it. They are enslaved to sin and either rationalize it or cover it up or live in defeat. This is the theme of our passage for today—Romans 6:1–14.

Understanding the Themes of Romans 6

Romans 6 is the Christian's emancipation proclamation. It is the foundational document declaring our freedom from Satan's intimidation and sin's domination. It is where we learn how to live free from fear, guilt, shame, and defeat.

> What shall we say then? Are we to continue in sin that grace might increase? May it never be! How shall we who died to sin still live in it? Or do you not know that all of us who have been baptized into Christ Jesus have been baptized into His death? Therefore we have been buried with Him through baptism into death, in order that as Christ was raised from the dead through the glory of the Father, so we too might walk in newness of life. For if we have become united with Him in the likeness of His death,

certainly we shall be also in the likeness of His resurrection, knowing this, that our old self was crucified with Him, that our body of sin might be done away with, that we should no longer be slaves to sin; for he who has died is freed from sin. Now if we have died with Christ, we believe that we shall also live with Him, knowing that Christ, having been raised from the dead, is never to die again; death no longer is master over Him. For the death that He died, He died to sin, once for all; but the life that He lives, He lives to God. Even so consider yourselves to be dead to sin, but alive to God in Christ Jesus.

Therefore do not let sin reign in your mortal body that you should obey its lusts, and do not go on presenting the members of your body to sin as instruments of unrighteousness; but present yourselves to God as those alive from the dead, and your members as instruments of righteousness to God. For sin shall not be master over you, for you are not under law, but under grace. (vv. 1–14)

Two groups of people are highlighted in Romans 6. One: *those who don't claim their liberty and continue to live like slaves* (vv. 1–14). Two: *those who take their freedom too far and take advantage of liberty* (vv. 15–23). The first group nullifies grace. The second group abuses it. To both of these groups Paul stands up and protests: "May it never be!" (vv. 2, 15). The very thought of grace being treated this way horrifies the apostle. He recoils and says, in essence, "Perish the thought!" Then he poses a question to them: "How shall we who died to sin still live in it?" (v. 2). Or in the language of our analogy, "Why would an emancipated slave ever want to stay with a harsh plantation owner?"

Claiming Our Freedom over Sin

The point of Romans 6 is that the old sinful nature that once ruled over us has been ousted from office. But we must learn how to keep it from regaining power over our lives. Paul presents three techniques on how to do just that—something we must *know*, something we must *consider*, and something we must *present*.

Know

Let's begin with what we are to know.

> Or do you not know that all of us who have been baptized into Christ Jesus have been baptized into His death? . . . knowing this, that our old self was crucified with Him, that our body of sin might be done away with, that we should no longer be slaves to sin; . . . knowing that Christ, having been raised from the dead, is never to die again; death no longer is master over Him. (vv. 3, 6, 9)

The baptism referred to in verse 3 is not water baptism but a dry baptism, not a physical one but a spiritual one (see 1 Cor. 10:1–2).

The word *baptism* comes from the Greek term *baptizō*, primarily meaning "identification." It was a term used in the first century for dipping a garment into dye. The act of dipping, which changed the identity of the cloth, was called *baptizō*.

When Christ died on the cross and arose from the tomb, He was dipped or baptized into death (Luke 12:50). As a result of the Resurrection, His perishable body changed to an imperishable one (1 Cor. 15:42–47). When we trusted in the Savior for eternal life, we became dipped into His death and resurrection. Similarly, our identity changed (2 Cor. 5:17). We didn't see it, we didn't hear it, we didn't feel it. But it changed nevertheless. His death to sin became our death to sin; His awakening to a whole new realm of life became our awakening (Rom. 6:8–10). A victorious walk begins with *knowing* this fact. And whether you live as a victor or a victim is determined by how well you know it and believe it.

Consider

Besides something to *know*, there is also something we need to *consider*.

> Even so consider yourselves to be dead to sin, but alive to God in Christ Jesus. (v. 11)

The word *consider* comes from a Greek term meaning "to calculate, to take into account, to figure." It is an accounting term that means to enter figures into the ledger. And what is it we are to enter in the credit column of our thinking? We should record that since we are in Christ, we are dead to sin's power; and being in Christ, we are alive with God's new power.

The bottom line of such calculations is found in verse 12.

> "Therefore do not let sin reign in your mortal body that you should obey its lusts."

The Pacific Coast Highway is a picturesque stretch of road that ribbons its way over the craggy California coastline. A few of the curves and drop-offs are treacherous. But they add both danger and grandeur to the journey. The state could offer two options to travelers along these dangerous mountain roads. They could either build well-equipped trauma centers at the bottom of the precipitous drop-offs, or they could plant warning signs at the critical junctions: Danger! Curve Ahead . . . Drive Slowly.

Romans 6 abounds with road signs: Danger Ahead! . . . No Need to Crash . . . Slow Down. And if we carefully consider them, our spiritual journey will be safe and scenic. But if we do crash through a guardrail, there is a trauma center called forgiveness at the base of the hill (1 John 1:9).

Present

This brings us to our third crucial term: *present.*

> And do not go on presenting the members of your body to sin as instruments of unrighteousness; but present yourselves to God as those alive from the dead, and your members as instruments of righteousness to God. For sin shall not be master over you, for you are not under law, but under grace. (Rom. 6:13– 14)

Not only must we make intelligent calculations based on the truth we know, we must also make a conscious presentation of ourselves to God. Paul spells this out in two commands—one stated negatively, one positively.

Negatively: "Do not go on presenting the members of your body to sin as instruments of unrighteousness." Why? Because we're no longer slaves. We're no longer living on the plantation. We've been emancipated.

Positively: "Present yourselves to God as those alive from the dead . . . for sin shall not be master over you." Since our old master has been run off, it's ludicrous that we should run after him to indenture ourselves to his service again. Instead, we should present ourselves to our new Master and embrace Him for the freedom He has given us.

Taking a Necessary Warning to Heart

In spite of the fact that the plantation economy was part of a civilization gone with the wind of the Civil War, plantation owners were determined to keep their newly freed slaves. Satan has that same determination, in spite of the victory won at the Cross.

In order for you to leave the security of your old way of life, you will need courage to walk into freedom's fields, into the amber waves of grace. You will need an inner resolve to walk tall, to walk free, and to never look back in longing for that old way of life. You will need a grace awakening.

Shortly after Congress passed the Emancipation Proclamation in 1863, Abraham Lincoln warned:

> We are like whalers who have been on a long chase.
> We have, at last, got the harpoon into the monster,
> but we must now look how we steer, or with one
> "flop" of his tail he will send us all into eternity.[4]

With those words, the president proved himself a prophet. His proclamation led to an escalation in the war. The impaling of freedom's harpoon brought a flailing response from the gray whale of the Confederacy. Many of you who have just plunged your iron barb into the breaching whale of legalism know the feeling. Suddenly you find the rope coiled at your feet spinning wildly over the bow of your boat. And now you find yourself towed relentlessly through the water by this leviathan of the deep.

A parting word of advice. Defeating legalism is going to be a rough ride, so hold on . . . and watch out for that tail!

 *Living Insights*   STUDY ONE

Romans 3:10–20 describes the squalor of our enslaved condition before Christ came into our lives and proclaimed us free. That description, however, is for humanity in general. In the space provided,

---

4. Henry J. Raymond, *The Life, Public Services, and State Papers of Abraham Lincoln* (New York, N.Y.: Darvy and Miller, 1865), p. 752.

describe the conditions of your own personal slavery before Jesus set you free.

_____

_____

_____

_____

_____

_____

_____

_____

Like Lot's wife, we sometimes look back on the Sodom and Gomorrah that lies over our shoulder. In spite of the fire and brimstone we see raining from the sky, we occasionally mourn the loss of those city sins that enslaved us.

Be honest now, is there anything you have walked away from when Christ called you out of Sin City that you're now looking at over your shoulder, regretful to have left it behind?

_____

_____

_____

Unless your goal in life is to become a salt lick, you need to stop looking back and longing for that old way of life.

Read Ephesians 4:17–32, and write down any advice that applies specifically to those things in your life that should be left behind.

_____

_____

_____

_____

List some specific sins or legalistic tendencies that you are enslaved to.

_____   _____

_____   _____

_____   _____

Now paraphrase Romans 6:1–14 in a personal way by writing a letter to yourself that urges you to give up those things. We'll start you off by doing the first two verses for you. You're on your own for the rest.

Dear _____,
(fill in your name)

What are you doing? Are you trying to show how gracious God is by griming up your life with sin? Do you have the mind of a pig, or what? Why would you want to wallow around in the mud when you just got out of the bath? . . .

_____

_____

_____

_____

_____

_____

_____

_____

_____

_____

_____

Chapter 7

GUIDING OTHERS TO FREEDOM
Romans 6:15–23 and Selected Scriptures

During the 1988 presidential election an unexpected shift of attention occurred. Instead of the evening news focusing on the candidates, all eyes were on three gray whales that were cut off from their migratory route by a frozen sea of ice.

At first, only a few Eskimos with chain saws attempted to rescue them. But when the media brought the whales' plight into our living rooms, volunteers flocked to the scene with heavy machinery and a determination to set those stranded whales free.

But the volunteers' ingenuity and energy were soon exhausted. Enter the National Guard. Their helicopters dropped a five-ton concrete basher to break up the ice. Then, in a cooperative effort with the United States, the Soviet Union dispatched two of their ice-breaking ships to facilitate the rescue.

After three weeks and an expenditure of one-and-a-half million dollars, the whales were freed. The heroic and noble rescue sparked a sense of compassion throughout the world. But it did something else too. By showing how willing we were to save a couple of ocean-going mammals, it underscored how hesitant we are to join hands in rescue efforts that involve mankind.

How many people would have pitched in to help some homeless couple stranded on the icy streets of Chicago? How many would have dug into their pockets to free a family from a New York ghetto? How many would have opened their homes to an unwed mother?

So willing to save the whales. So reluctant to save our fellow human beings.

Unfortunately, that same reluctance can be found within the family of God. Many people are quick to want to free some heathen halfway around the world from the shackles of sin, yet they are pathetically slow to raise a finger to loose other Christians from the chains of legalism.

Wonderful Truths regarding Freedom

What these shackled people need is a helicopter to come and

drop some five-ton concrete bashers to break up the ice that hems them in. They need to be liberated from legalism—so they can breathe. Here are a few passages of Scripture that help do just that.

> It was for freedom that Christ set us free; therefore keep standing firm and do not be subject again to a yoke of slavery. (Gal. 5:1)

> For he who has died is freed from sin. (Rom. 6:7)

> For the law of the Spirit of life in Christ Jesus has set you free from the law of sin and of death. (8:2)

> What then shall we say to these things? If God is for us, who is against us? He who did not spare His own Son, but delivered Him up for us all, how will He not also with Him freely give us all things? (vv. 31–32)

> "And you shall know the truth, and the truth shall make you free. . . . If therefore the Son shall make you free, you shall be free indeed." (John 8:32, 36)

These breathing holes in Scripture give us the air we need to stay alive spiritually. In 1 Corinthians 10:25–30, Paul breaks open another hole in the cold, hard, legalistic ice that would entrap us.

> Eat anything that is sold in the meat market, without asking questions for conscience' sake; for the earth is the Lord's, and all it contains. If one of the unbelievers invites you, and you wish to go, eat anything that is set before you, without asking questions for conscience' sake. But if anyone should say to you, "This is meat sacrificed to idols," do not eat it, for the sake of the one who informed you, and for conscience' sake; I mean not your own conscience, but the other man's; for why is my freedom judged by another's conscience? If I partake with thankfulness, why am I slandered concerning that for which I give thanks?

In Paul's day Christians didn't wrestle with questions about dancing or going to movies. They wrestled with whether or not they should eat meat that had been offered to idols.

In pagan worship, portions of meat were sacrificed to idols, and the part of the animal that was left over was sold to a meat market.

Many Christians had reservations about eating the leftovers from these pagan rituals—especially those who had just converted from idol worship to Christianity.

How did Paul handle this situation? Did he ice up the harbor with a lot of rigid, pharisaical instructions? No. He broke open a breathing hole. He said they were free to eat (vv. 25–27). The only time he limited that freedom was when there was a risk of violating someone else's conscience (vv. 28–29, 32–33).

God has given His children a wonderful freedom in Christ, which includes not only freedom from sin and shame but also freedom from living under a legalistic lifestyle imposed by other Christians. Yet that doesn't imply that we are to run footloose and fancy-free, trampling over the garden in someone else's backyard. No. There are some fences that limit our freedom. And two of those fences are found in Romans 6, erected in the form of questions.

First Fence to Freedom

Earlier in Romans 5:20 Paul said, "Where sin increased, grace abounded all the more." Romans 6:1 poses the question that would logically flow from that assertion.

> What shall we say then? Are we to continue in
> sin that grace might increase?

The people who would raise this question are those who have failed to live in freedom. They live their lives overly sensitive to sin. As a result, sin dominates their lives and a sense of shame binds them. Paul answers their question with the good news that they've been set free from their old master. All they have to do is step out of the shackles that Christ has already unlocked.

Talk about opening up breathing holes! With words of grace like that, we should be out in the expansive ocean, swimming free and unhindered.

Second Fence to Freedom

The second question looks the same as the first, but on closer inspection this fence is really quite different.

> What then? Shall we sin because we are not
> under law but under grace? May it never be! (v. 15)

In other words, if there are no policemen lurking behind the speed limit signs, why not rev up the RPMs and go full throttle?

But that would be abusing grace, and it really wouldn't be living in freedom either. Liberty without limits is like an elementary school parking lot without speed bumps. If we live by grace, we should not be drag racing in wanton disregard of the safety of school children. We should drive conscientiously, always having our foot ready to hit the brakes should a pedestrian step into our way.

Careful Warnings to All Who Are Free

Even those who live in a free country need warnings. So we shouldn't be surprised that God gives a few warnings of His own, lest we abuse our privileges as people under grace. These warnings are set forth in Romans 6:16–23. But first we want to look at an overall principle that is woven throughout this section, and which is specifically found in verse 16.

> Do you not know that when you present yourselves
> to someone as slaves for obedience, you are slaves
> of the one whom you obey, either of sin resulting in
> death, or of obedience resulting in righteousness?

The principle is this: *How we live depends on the master we choose.* Before our relationship with Christ, we were all trapped under the ice. Breathing free wasn't an option. There was no way we could find freedom, no way to enjoy the crisp air of righteousness. But grace freed us from the requirement to serve sin, allowing us the opportunity to follow Christ's directives voluntarily. So as long as we do this, we will not sin. Though we may lapse into sin, we don't have to let it dominate our lives on a day-to-day basis, because grace has given us the freedom to obey.

> But thanks be to God that though you were slaves
> of sin, you became obedient from the heart to that
> form of teaching to which you were committed, and
> having been freed from sin, you became slaves of
> righteousness. (vv. 17–18)

When someone deliberately decides to disobey, that person isn't living free. In fact, those defiant decisions do just the opposite. They bind and constrict.

> His own iniquities will capture the wicked,
> And he will be held with the cords of his sin.

He will die for lack of instruction,
And in the greatness of his folly he will go astray.
(Prov. 5:22–23)

So our first warning is: *Never hide behind grace as a cover for disobedience.* Any prodigal can excuse life in a pigsty by saying, "It doesn't matter how much mud I wallow in; it's all under grace." But grace doesn't mean we're free to live any way we want. It means we're free to become everything God created us to be. Under grace, we're free to choose what path we take—the path of righteousness or the path of disobedience. But if we make too many of the wrong choices, the path can become dark with regret and overgrown with the tendrils of thorny consequences.

William Barclay writes about that dead-end path.

> Sin begets sin. The first time we do a wrong thing, we may do it with hesitation and a tremor and a shudder. The second time we do it, it is easier; and if we go on doing it, it becomes effortless; sin loses its terror. . . . To start on the path of sin is to go on to more and more.[1]

Another writer describes this dark, downward path in greater detail.

> One lie had to be covered by a dozen more. . . .
>
> The downward cycle of sin moved from a problem to a faulty sinful response, thereby causing an additional complicating problem which was met by an additional sinful response. . . .
>
> . . . Sinful habits are hard to break, but if they are not broken they will bind the client ever more tightly. He is held fast by these ropes. . . . At length, he becomes sin's slave.[2]

What if that describes you?

What if you've strayed from the path of righteousness? What if you've wandered down the primrose path of your passions only to find that it leads to a briar patch? What then?

1. William Barclay, *The Letter to the Romans*, rev. ed., The Daily Study Bible Series (Philadelphia, Pa.: Westminster Press, 1975), pp. 90–91.

2. Jay E. Adams, *Competent to Counsel* (Phillipsburg, N.J.: Presbyterian and Reformed Publishing Co., 1970), p. 145.

Grace doesn't prevent you from falling and breaking your leg as you walk down that path. Neither does it keep you from becoming entangled in some thorny situations. But grace will let you repent of the wrong and help you find your way back to the right path.

And that's good news to people who have fallen headlong down the wrong path, people with skinned knees who are trying to pick themselves up, tears streaming down their faces.

Which brings us to our second warning: *We cannot live by grace without guidance.* Even though our nature yearns to be free, the indisputable fact is, we need a master. We need someone to guide our steps down the paths of righteousness (Ps. 23:3). We have such a guide, such a master, in Jesus, whose costly death gave us the option of living free.

> I am speaking in human terms because of the weakness of your flesh. For just as you presented your members as slaves to impurity and to lawlessness, resulting in further lawlessness, so now present your members as slaves to righteousness, resulting in sanctification. For when you were slaves of sin, you were free in regard to righteousness. Therefore what benefit were you then deriving from the things of which you are now ashamed? For the outcome of those things is death. But now having been freed from sin and enslaved to God, you derive your benefit, resulting in sanctification, and the outcome, eternal life. For the wages of sin is death, but the free gift of God is eternal life in Christ Jesus our Lord. (Rom. 6:19–23)

These verses say two things. First: *Make the right choice* (vv. 19–21). Second: *Focus on the benefits of your current position in grace* (vv. 22–23).

Because of God's grace we are free from sin's mastery. *By* God's grace we are enslaved to God. *Through* God's grace there are benefits to be derived. And what are those benefits? At least three come immediately to mind: (1) the exciting process of growing to maturity as a Christian, (2) a guilt-free lifestyle characterized by creativity and freedom, and (3) the joyful outcome of eternal life.

Contrast those benefits with the wages that the harsh taskmaster of sin doles out: (1) an instant breakdown of fellowship with God (Isa. 59:2), (2) the removal of God's blessing (Deut. 28), (3) the misery of a guilty conscience (Ps. 32:3–4), (4) loss of personal integrity (2 Sam. 12:1–12; 16:5–8), (5) sudden stoppage of spiritual growth (1 Kings 11:1–4), (6) strained relationships with fellow Christians (1 Cor. 5:9–13). The payoff from sin's outturned pockets looks pretty depressing, doesn't it?

Helpful Reminders That Keep Us Balanced

As we conclude this lesson, we want to tie a couple of strings around your finger as reminders of the balance that is necessary to walk with Christ.

First: *Abusing grace stagnates us.* It dulls our spiritual taste buds to the sweetness of God. It causes us to live casual, indifferent lives, instead of committed ones. What's worse, when we live stagnated lives, we lead others astray. As a result, our lives become an embarrassment to the kingdom rather than an exemplification of its King.

Second: *Living in freedom motivates us.* It motivates us to let go. When we're not free, we want to control others and the circumstances around us. But when we're operating in a grace state of mind, we release others to make their own decisions about their life and lifestyle, and we free ourselves to accept each day as it comes. The following poem says it best.

To "Let Go" Takes Love

> To "let go" does not mean to stop caring, it
>   means that I can't do it for someone else.
> To "let go" is not to cut myself off, it is the
>   realization that I can't control another.
> To "let go" is not to enable, but to allow learning
>   from natural consequences.
> To "let go" is to admit powerlessness, which means
>   the outcome is not in my hands.
> To "let go" is not to try to change or blame
>   another, it is to make the most of myself.
> To "let go" is not to care for, but to care about.
> To "let go" is not to fix, but to be supportive.
> To "let go" is not to judge, but to allow another to
>   be a human being.
> To "let go" is not to be in the middle arranging
>   all the outcomes but to allow others to effect
>   their own destinies.
> To "let go" is not to be protective, it is to permit

another to face reality.

To "let go" is not to deny, but to accept.

To "let go" is not to nag, scold, or argue, but instead to search out my own shortcomings and to correct them.

To "let go" is not to adjust everything to my desires but to take each day as it comes, and to cherish myself in it.

To "let go" is not to criticize and regulate anybody but to try to become what I dream I can be.

To "let go" is not to regret the past, but to grow and to live for the future.

To "let go" is to fear less and to love more.[3]

 ## _Living Insights_

Our study for today shines a light on the two paths that stretch before us: the path of sin and the path of righteousness. The former belongs to our old taskmaster. The latter belongs to our new master, the Lord Jesus.

Look up Job 18:5–11; Proverbs 3:13–26; 4:10–19 and 26–27; and Isaiah 26:7; and describe what you can expect somewhere down the road on these respective paths.

The Path of Sin	The Path of Righteousness

3. "To 'Let Go' Takes Love," quoted by Margaret J. Rinck in _Can Christians Love Too Much?_ (Grand Rapids, Mich.: Zondervan Publishing House, Pyranee Books, 1989), p. 157.

_____ _____

_____ _____

_____ _____

Which road do you find yourself on?_____

If you're on the path of sin and want to get back to having fellowship with God, read Luke 15:11–24 to find directions for the way home.

If you're on the path of righteousness but are taking pride in how you've kept on the straight and narrow, read Luke 18:9–14 to get your bearings.

If you're on the path of righteousness and walking humbly behind your Master, turn to the compass reading in Micah 6:8 and use it to keep your bearings straight.

 Living Insights _____

Take the poem at the end of the lesson and turn it into a prayer list for your personal needs. For example, the theme of the poem is letting go, so begin your prayer something like this: *"Dear Lord, please teach me how to let go . . ."*

The first line of the poem is: "To 'let go' does not mean to stop caring, it means that I can't do it for someone else." Turn this into a petition to God by praying something like this: *"Please help me realize what it means to let go—and what it doesn't mean. It doesn't mean I stop caring. It means I can't crowd other people's lives and do everything for them."*

Now, take it a step further. Make the prayer specific. Take that same thought in the first line of the poem and apply it to someone to whom you're having a hard time giving freedom. For example: *"Lord, help me let go of _____. I know I'm crowding _____'s life and trespassing in areas that I shouldn't be. Help me care for _____ in such a way that I don't tread upon _____'s self-respect. Specifically, Lord, help me back away from doing . . ."*

Chapter 8
THE GRACE TO
LET OTHERS BE
Romans 14

To cover this expansive subject of grace sufficiently, we need to address both vertical and horizontal grace . . . the amazing grace that holds out hope to sinners and the liberating grace that gives people room to breathe. In our first several lessons we took the time to examine God's unmerited grace toward us. Today we'll look at grace as it flows toward one another.

How are you at demonstrating God's grace to others, at giving others breathing room? Do you lessen other people's guilt, or do you add to it? Do you promote liberty, or do you restrain it?

These questions have to do with attitude, don't they? Depending on whether our attitude is gracious or rigid, liberty or legalism will be the result. Dr. Viktor Frankl talks about the importance of attitude in his book *Man's Search for Meaning*.

> We who lived in concentration camps can remember the men who walked through the huts comforting others, giving away their last piece of bread. They may have been few in number, but they offer sufficient proof that everything can be taken from a man but one thing: the last of the human freedoms—to choose one's attitude in any given set of circumstances. . . .
>
> And there were always choices to make. Every day, every hour, offered the opportunity to make a decision, a decision which determined whether you would or would not submit to those powers which threatened to rob you of your very self, your inner freedom; which determined whether or not you would become the plaything of circumstance, renouncing freedom and dignity to become molded into the form of the typical inmate. . . .
>
> . . . Even though conditions such as lack of sleep, insufficient food and various mental stresses may suggest that the inmates were bound to react in certain ways, in the final analysis it becomes clear

that the sort of person the prisoner became was the result of an inner decision, and not the result of camp influences alone.[1]

It is those inner decisions, more than outer influences, that mold us into the people we are. In today's lesson we want to uncover those attitudes that keep us from living out the promise of grace. And we want to discover the attitudes that will help us extend the kind of grace that lets others be whoever and whatever God is leading them to be.

Two Strong Tendencies That Nullify Grace

Located in one of the great doctrinal books of the Bible is a series of commands that, if obeyed, would turn us into some of the most affirming people imaginable.

> Let love be without hypocrisy. Abhor what is evil; cling to what is good. Be devoted to one another in brotherly love; give preference to one another in honor; not lagging behind in diligence, fervent in spirit, serving the Lord; rejoicing in hope, persevering in tribulation, devoted to prayer, contributing to the needs of the saints, practicing hospitality. Bless those who persecute you; bless and curse not. Rejoice with those who rejoice, and weep with those who weep. Be of the same mind toward one another; do not be haughty in mind, but associate with the lowly. Do not be wise in your own estimation. Never pay back evil for evil to anyone. Respect what is right in the sight of all men. (Rom. 12:9–17)

In a nutshell, these words represent the essence of authentic Christianity. But why don't we live authentic lives? Why do we love with such hypocrisy? What keeps us from being devoted to one another, from honoring one another, from contributing to each other's needs?

The inescapable fact is that, more often than not, we nullify grace rather than magnify it. We resist it more often than we release it. What is it within us that hinders an attitude of free-flowing grace?

Most of us fall short of letting others be themselves because of

1. Viktor E. Frankl, *Man's Search for Meaning* (New York, N.Y.: Pocket Books, 1963), pp. 104–5.

two strong and very human tendencies: *We compare ourselves with others*, which leads us to criticize or compete with them, and *we attempt to control others*, which results in our manipulating and intimidating them. Let's dissect and examine both of these tendencies that keep grace from awakening in our lives.

To Compare

Most people tend to prefer sameness, predictability, and common interests. As a result, if someone thinks differently, prefers different entertainment, wears different clothes, or enjoys a different lifestyle, we get a little nervous.

Our problem is one of eyesight. We tend to see things only on the surface, and therefore, we put too much weight on externals. We judge by appearances rather than actualities.

But the problem is deeper than that. It goes beyond the need for an eye exam. We need an attitude adjustment—because comparison knocks our attitude out of alignment. It makes us prejudiced people. And it counteracts and opposes the work of grace.

God never meant for the church to be a religious industry designed to churn out cookie-cutter Christians and paper-doll saints. On the contrary, His church is supposed to be a celebration of diversity (see 1 Cor. 12).

Unsure of this? Look at the people in the Bible. They are as different as Rahab and Esther, the one an ex-prostitute and the other an exquisite queen.

Variety honors God. Uniformity bores Him. Consider how variegated are the threads woven through the genealogy of God's Son in Matthew. Cup your ears in the marble hallways of faith in Hebrews 11 and hear the echoes of diversity. Page through church history and read about the great differences in the men and women who shaped the world.

Legalism requires that we all be alike, unified in convictions and uniform in appearance. Grace finds pleasure in our diversity, encourages individuality, and leaves room for differences of opinion. But before we will be able to demonstrate sufficient grace to let others be who they are, we'll have to get rid of this legalistic tendency to compare.

To Control

Another attitude we need to change is the desire to control others. This tendency is especially prevalent among those who find their security in religious rigidity. They manipulate by using fear tactics, veiled threats, and oblique hints to get their way. Controllers win by intimidation. Whether physical or verbal, their ways are those of the schoolyard bully.

Whatever the method, controlling, like comparing, nullifies grace.

Some Biblical Guidelines That Magnify Grace

But we don't want to dwell on those things that nullify grace. We want to discover those things that magnify it.

Further on in his letter to the Romans, Paul goes into great detail regarding the issue of personal freedom. In the fourteenth chapter, for example, he sets forth four practical guidelines to help us release others in grace. The first guideline is found in verses 1–4.

Accept Others

> Now accept the one who is weak in faith, but not for the purpose of passing judgment on his opinions. One man has faith that he may eat all things, but he who is weak eats vegetables only. Let not him who eats regard with contempt him who does not eat, and let not him who does not eat judge him who eats, for God has accepted him. Who are you to judge the servant of another? To his own master he stands or falls; and stand he will, for the Lord is able to make him stand.

Guideline one: *Accepting others is basic to letting them be.* The problem in Romans 14 was not a food problem. It was a love problem, an *acceptance* problem. It still is. How often do we restrict our love by making it conditional? How often do we make our acceptance dependent upon how others measure up to our own set of expectations?

Whether it's the meat sacrificed in a heathen temple or the movie showing in a Hollywood theater, the principle is the same: *Accept one another.*

When we don't accept one another, conflicts arise, and Paul pinpoints the two most common ways that people react to these conflicts. First he says, "Let not him who eats regard with contempt him who does not eat" (v. 3a). The words *regard with contempt* mean "to regard as nothing, utterly despise, to discount entirely." Second he says, "Let not him who does not eat judge him who eats" (v. 3b). The word *judge* means "to criticize, to view negatively, to make assumptions that are exaggerated, erroneous, and even damaging to character."

No matter how strongly we may feel about a certain cultural taboo, judging another who disagrees with us or looking down our nose with contempt is wrong.

Why? Because, as verse 4 indicates, another person's convictions are none of our business. After all, who made us the judge to pass a verdict on other people's lifestyles? Who made us the judge to mete out the sentence of condemnation?

It's God's job to direct them. It's our job to accept them. Then what all does acceptance entail?

> It means you are valuable just as you are. It allows you to be the *real* you. You aren't forced into someone else's idea of who you really are. It means your ideas are taken seriously since they reflect you. You can talk about how you feel inside and why you feel that way—and someone really cares.
>
> Acceptance means you can try out your ideas without being shot down. You can even express heretical thoughts and discuss them with intelligent questioning. You feel safe. No one will pronounce judgment on you, even though they don't agree with you. It doesn't mean you will never be corrected or shown to be wrong; it simply means it is safe to be *you* and no one will destroy *you* out of prejudice.[2]

Acceptance is basic to letting others be themselves. Consider the next four verses of Romans 14 as we turn to a second guideline.

Let Others Decide for Themselves

> One man regards one day above another, another regards every day alike. Let each man be fully convinced in his own mind. He who observes the day, observes it for the Lord, and he who eats, does so for the Lord, for he gives thanks to God; and he who eats not, for the Lord he does not eat, and gives thanks to God. For not one of us lives for himself, and not one dies for himself; for if we live, we live for the Lord, or if we die, we die for the Lord; therefore whether we live or die, we are the Lord's. (vv. 5–8)

2. Gladys M. Hunt, "That's No Generation Gap!" *Eternity Magazine*, October 1969, p. 15.

Guideline two: *Refusing to dictate to others allows the Lord freedom to direct their lives.* Do you want to help others grow to maturity? Here's how. Let them grow up differently. Let them unfold to blossom at their own pace and in their own way. Let them decide for themselves. Let them have the freedom to fail and learn from their own mistakes.

Each of us belongs to the Lord, Paul states in verse 8. When we realize that, we will stop dictating and start trusting the Lord to direct the steps of His children.

Refuse to Judge Others

The third guideline is found in verses 9–12.

> For to this end Christ died and lived again, that He might be Lord both of the dead and of the living. But you, why do you judge your brother? Or you again, why do you regard your brother with contempt? For we shall all stand before the judgment seat of God. For it is written,
> "As I live, says the Lord, every knee shall
>   bow to Me,
> And every tongue shall give praise to God."
> So then each one of us shall give account of himself to God.

Guideline three: *Freeing others means we never assume a position we're not qualified to fill.* What keeps us from being qualified to judge? Several things.

Not being omniscient, we don't know all the facts. Unable to see into people's hearts, we can't read motives. Being finite, we lack "the big picture." Having poor spiritual eyesight, we live with blind spots and blurred perspectives. Most of all, being human, we are imperfect, inconsistent, and subjective.

Does this guideline mean we must always agree with each other? Certainly not. But it does mean we should be civil in our conflicts.

Express Your Liberty Wisely

The final guideline flows out of verses 13–18.

> Therefore let us not judge one another anymore, but rather determine this—not to put an obstacle or a stumbling block in a brother's way. I know and am convinced in the Lord Jesus that nothing is unclean

in itself; but to him who thinks anything to be unclean, to him it is unclean. For if because of food your brother is hurt, you are no longer walking according to love. Do not destroy with your food him for whom Christ died. Therefore do not let what is for you a good thing be spoken of as evil; for the kingdom of God is not eating and drinking, but righteousness and peace and joy in the Holy Spirit. For he who in this way serves Christ is acceptable to God and approved by men.

Guideline four: *Loving others requires us to express our liberty wisely.* In other words, love must rule. Our goal is not to please ourselves — or others — but the Lord (2 Cor. 5:9, 15). He is the one who bought us with His blood.

Consequently, we shouldn't act out our lives according to what others say. Rather, we should act out our lives on the basis of our love for others because we answer to Christ (v. 10).

One way to show our love for others is by expressing our liberty wisely. We do that by enjoying our liberty without flaunting it . . . quietly, privately, and with those of like mind who aren't offended by the liberty.

A Few Actions That Signify Grace

We want to conclude our discussion today with a few thoughts culled from Romans 14:19.

So then let us pursue the things which make for peace and the building up of one another.

On the basis of this statement, consider a few actions that signify grace.

1. *Concentrate on things that encourage peace and assist other's growth.* Filter whatever you do through this twofold grid: Is this going to encourage peace? and, Is this going to hurt and offend or help and strengthen?

2. *Remember that sabotaging saints hurts the work of God.* Paul warns in verse 20 not to "tear down the work of God for the sake of food." You sabotage the saints when you flaunt your liberty, knowing that others have convictions against it. Enjoy your liberty, but enjoy it discreetly.

3. *Exercise your liberty only with those who can enjoy it with you.* That means to keep it private and personal. That's not deception. It's wise and necessary restraint.

4. *Determine where you stand and refuse to play God in anyone else's life.* By letting others be, you free yourself to give full attention to what God is trying to make of you. When you're totally absorbed with that, you won't have the time or the energy to hold on to somebody else's life.

 ## L*iv*ing I*n*sights

Romans 14 is a chapter not about issues central to the faith but about peripheral things like meat sacrificed to idols and the observance of religious days. Paul's point is that these peripheral issues shouldn't cause division.

The body of Christ should have unity *and* diversity. It should not only incorporate a diversity of gifts (1 Cor. 12), but it should tolerate a diversity of opinions (Rom. 14).

That principle holds just as true today as it did almost two thousand years ago. The following is a list of contemporary issues, all peripheral. What are your convictions about these gray-area issues? How were these convictions formed in your life—parental influence, peers, childhood experiences, church teachings?

Movies _____

_____

Television _____

_____

Cosmetics _____

_____

Clothes _____

_____

Going to a restaurant that sells liquor _____

_____

Cosmetic surgery _____

_____

Birth control _____

_____

Having a daily quiet time _____

_____

Music _____

_____

Dancing _____

_____

Drinking _____

_____

The lottery _____

_____

Now search through the Bible to support your convictions with Scripture.

Movies _____

_____

Television _____

_____

Cosmetics _____

_____

Clothes _____

_____

Going to a restaurant that sells liquor _____

_____

Cosmetic surgery _____

_____

Birth control _____

_____

Having a daily quiet time _____

_____

Music _____

_____

Dancing _____

_____

Drinking _____

_____

The lottery _____

_____

🌹 *Living Insights* STUDY TWO

Of the convictions you listed in Study One, which ones cause the most divisiveness in your relationships with others?

_____

_____

What could you do to demonstrate more tolerance with others whose convictions are different from yours?

_____

_____

_____

_____

_____

Look up the following references, and jot down some principles concerning your relationship with those within the body of Christ.

Romans 15:7 _____

_____

_____

1 Thessalonians 5:14, compared with Hebrews 12:12–13 _____

_____

_____

_____

Matthew 5:9; Hebrews 12:14; Romans 12:18 _____

_____

_____

_____

_____

Romans 14:19 _____

_____

_____

Galatians 5:22–23 _____

_____

_____

Chapter 9

GRACIOUSLY DISAGREEING AND PRESSING ON

Acts 15:36–41; Ephesians 4:29–32

O ne of the marks of maturity is the ability to disagree without becoming disagreeable. And that takes grace. In fact, handling disagreements with tact is one of the crowning achievements of grace.

Unfortunately, it seems that the older we get the more stingy we become in giving grace to others. This is especially true of those of us in the evangelical community. You would think that the church would be the one place a person could find tolerance, tact, open-mindedness, and plenty of room for disagreement. But it's not. The doors are most often closed to differing points of view.

And more often than not these differences give rise to dissension. There are wonderful exceptions, of course; but when most Christians disagree, they do so in a blunt and tactless way, sometimes even in an accusatory and sarcastic way.

Ephesians 4:29 offers a bit of corrective advice to such people.

> Let no unwholesome word proceed from your mouth, but only such a word as is good for edification according to the need of the moment, that it may give grace to those who hear.

"That it may give grace to those who hear." What a goal! What an incentive to clean up our critical attitudes and speak the truth in love!

Things We Agree on regarding Disagreements

Even if we do pursue peace, and even if we are as positive and as tactful as we can be, disagreements will still arise. The following are four things most of us would agree on regarding disagreements.

1. *Disagreements are inevitable.* Pick any subject and you will find people perched on either side of the fence. Animal rights. Capital punishment. The environment. If you're for it, you can bet someone else is against it. Because we are so diverse, differences are bound to arise. But that's what freedom is all about— respecting other people's differences, whether those differences

are racial, political, or ideological. That's what religious freedom is all about. And even though our theological persuasion may not bend, our involvement with others must. There must be "wobble room" that allows for differences.

2. *Even the godly will sometimes disagree.* For some, it's difficult to understand how two people who passionately love the Lord and His Word could stand diametrically opposed on certain issues. But they can. Consider the confrontation between Paul and Barnabas in Acts 15:36–41, which we will be studying in more detail in our lesson today. Fortunately, when we get to heaven, we will be a renewed body of believers living in perfect harmony with each other. But until then, we will disagree on occasion— even the most godly of us.

3. *In every disagreement there will be the same two ingredients: an issue and various viewpoints.* The issue involves principles and is usually objective. The viewpoints involve personalities and are usually subjective. Therein lies the source of most every clash— a disagreement on an issue because of opposing points of view. Understanding these two simple ingredients will help you keep calm and collected in a conflict with others. Why? The next fact will explain.

4. *In many disagreements each side is valid.* Differing viewpoints are not so much an "I am right and you are wrong" matter as they are an "I see it from this perspective, and you see it from that perspective" matter. Both sides of most disagreements have strengths and weaknesses, which means neither side is airtight in its logic or ironclad in its conclusions. Nevertheless, any disagreement can lead to division; any conflict can create a rift in a relationship.

A Disagreement between Two Godly Leaders

Sometimes God uses a major disagreement between two capable servants of His to spread the gospel in different directions. That is exactly what happened with Paul and Barnabas. Two more dedicated, more godly men couldn't have been found in the first century. Both were effective and spiritually minded. Neither was selfish or immature. But what sparks flew when those two men of spiritual steel clashed!

Let's look now into the biblical account and set the stage for the tremor that shook those two pillars of the New Testament church. It all started when they took their first missionary journey together. Accompanying those two well-rooted men of the faith was a young man named John Mark, a mere sapling of a saint, who was Barnabas' cousin.

> And when they reached Salamis, they began to pro-
> claim the word of God in the synagogues of the Jews;
> and they also had John as their helper. (Acts 13:5)

When the team trudged through Pamphylia, they reached an imposing range of mountains that stood before them like strong-shouldered giants of stone. To make matters worse, the coastline was infested with malaria-carrying mosquitoes. Needless to say, when they reached Perga in Pamphylia, the honeymoon of adventure had become totally eclipsed. Perhaps he lost heart. Perhaps he grew homesick. Whatever the reason, John Mark had had enough of missionary life.

> Now Paul and his companions put out to sea
> from Paphos and came to Perga in Pamphylia; and
> John left them and returned to Jerusalem. (v. 13)

John Mark's missionary dream had turned into a major nightmare. When the going got tough, he got tired. Just when they all needed to pull together, he pulled out. His timing couldn't have been worse. It's very possible that Paul had gone down for the count after a bout with malaria or migraines from an eye disease. Later on the trip, Paul was stoned and left for dead.

The Critical Issue

Sometime after returning from that first journey, Paul wanted to see how those churches were doing, so he planned a return trip. That's when the disagreement happened.

> And after some days Paul said to Barnabas, "Let
> us return and visit the brethren in every city in
> which we proclaimed the word of the Lord, and see
> how they are." And Barnabas was desirous of taking
> John, called Mark, along with them also. But Paul
> kept insisting that they should not take him along
> who had deserted them in Pamphylia and had not
> gone with them to the work. (15:36–38)

Remember what we said earlier? In every disagreement there are two ingredients: an objective issue and an opposing viewpoint. The issue: Should a person who defects from a mission and leaves people in the lurch be given a second chance on a similar mission? The viewpoints: Paul said no, Barnabas said yes.

The Opposing Viewpoints

Each man was fully convinced he was right, because each viewed the issue from a different vantage point. Barnabas was people-oriented; Paul was more task-oriented. Barnabas was a man of compassion; Paul was a man of conviction. Barnabas was a builder of men; Paul was a planter of churches.

Paul looked at the issue from the viewpoint of the overall good of the ministry. Barnabas looked at the issue from the viewpoint of the overall good of the man.

A close examination of the text reveals the intensity of Paul's feelings. The Greek word translated "deserted" in verse 38 is a term from which we get the word *apostasized*. In Paul's mind John Mark had done more than jump ship; he had apostasized, he had been unfaithful.

To some of us, Paul may seem harsh and Barnabas greathearted. But before we side with Barnabas, let's look at a proverb that undoubtedly had popped into Paul's pragmatic mind:

> Like a bad tooth and an unsteady foot
> Is confidence in a faithless man in time of trouble.
> (Prov. 25:19)[1]

Paul had a point. But we're really not trying to get you to cast a vote for either viewpoint. We're just trying to get you to see both sides of the issue. It's hard to do that, though, when emotions are flaring—which is what was happening in verse 39.

> And there arose such a sharp disagreement that they separated from one another, and Barnabas took Mark with him and sailed away to Cyprus. (Acts 15:39)

1. The German scholar Franz Delitzsch amplifies the verse with this paraphrase: "He who in a time of need makes a faithless man his ground of confidence, is like one who seeks to bite with a broken tooth, and which he finally crushes, and one who supports himself on a shaking leg, and thus stumbles and falls." F. Delitzsch, *Proverbs*, in *Commentary on the Old Testament in Ten Volumes*, C. F. Keil and F. Delitzsch, trans. James Martin (reprint, Grand Rapids, Mich.: William B. Eerdmans Publishing Co., 1978), vol. 6, p. 165.

The Greek word for "sharp disagreement" is *paroxysm*. Interestingly, our English word "paroxysm" is transliterated letter for letter. Webster says *paroxysm* is "a fit, attack, or sudden increase or recurrence of symptoms (as of a disease)."[2] It is a convulsion, a violent emotion. Such a rift resulted from Paul and Barnabas' disagreement that the torn relationship could not be easily or quickly mended.

The final outcome? "They separated from one another."

The Permanent Separation

The two men went their separate ways and never ministered together again. If you take out a Bible atlas, you'll find that they trekked off in opposite directions. Barnabas and John Mark traveled the water route to Cyprus. Paul and his new partner, Silas, traveled the land route in a northeasterly direction to Syria, turning westward to Cilicia and the surrounding cities.

> But Paul chose Silas and departed, being committed
> by the brethren to the grace of the Lord. And he
> was traveling through Syria and Cilicia, strengthen-
> ing the churches. (vv. 40–41)

Keep in mind that Paul and Barnabas were longtime friends. Remember, Barnabas was the one who introduced the converted persecutor of the church to the Christian community (see Acts 9:19b–27). But in a fireworks display of emotion, their ministry together blew up in their faces.

Yet just as a violent storm leaves a nourishing rain in its wake, so also good things can result from a tempestuous falling out. Who knows what ministries grew up in Cyprus and blossomed in the regions beyond? Furthermore, it was John Mark who wrote the gospel of Mark.

Time healed the wounds of that closing encounter between Paul and Barnabas. Later in his life Paul wrote favorably of Barnabas (see 1 Cor. 9:6). He even wrote favorably of John Mark: "Pick up Mark and bring him with you, for he is useful to me for service" (2 Tim. 4:11b).

The best part of this story is that both of these strongly principled men got over their disagreement. In too many cases the battles go on and on, long after the dust of the original conflict has

---

2. *Webster's Ninth New Collegiate Dictionary*, see "paroxysm."

settled. How many people today are sitting in a stew of bitterness over past battles, still licking their wounds?

Disagreements are discouraging, but they need not be debilitating. Paul and Barnabas didn't spend the remainder of their lives getting back at each other. That takes grace.

Modeling Grace through Disagreeable Times

We will all encounter those with whom we disagree. We can't escape that. But we can learn to disagree graciously. Here are four suggestions to help you become a model of grace when those disagreeable times come.

First: *Always leave room for an opposing viewpoint.* A word for those of you with teenagers: If you don't have room for an opposing viewpoint, you're not going to fare well in weathering their adolescent years. During that time, teens can be quite vocal in their opposition. And what catches us off guard is that sometimes it's not rebellion; sometimes they're right! Their different point of view can, at worst, be challenging. At best, it can change our perspective.

Second: *If an argument must occur, don't assassinate.* An argument is one thing. Character assassination is another. If you have to put on boxing gloves and get in the ring, don't resort to hitting below the belt. If you must fight, fight fair.

Third: *If you don't get your way, get over it and get on with life.* If you wind up on the short end of the stick in a congregational vote, don't take your ball and pout all the way home. Get over it and get on with your life. Don't call for a recount or a referendum. Don't filibuster the congregation, droning on and on about your defeat. Life is too short to be petty and too precious to piddle it away pouting.

Fourth: *Sometimes the best solution is a separation.* The situation with Paul and Barnabas set a biblical precedent for this. They couldn't come to terms so they took to the road. If separation is the best solution, do it graciously. How do you know when it's time to put a little distance between you and the person you're having problems with? When your disagreements start to outweigh your agreements. Separation is never easy, but it may be God's way of moving you on to another dimension of ministry. That ministry may be the mountaintop experience of your life. Separation is merely the valley you have to go through to get there.

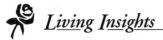

We've learned much from our passage today in Acts 15, which detailed the disagreement that arose between Paul and Barnabas. Now let's go further and investigate some other portions of Scripture that address this difficult issue of conflict.

What is Paul's advice in 1 Corinthians 1:10 about quarrels that arise within the body of Christ?

According to 3:1–3, what does strife within a church reveal?

From 11:18–19 what positive result arises out of conflicts?

How can divisions within the body of Christ be eliminated, according to 12:25?

How do you respond when someone opposes your viewpoint on something?

How can you disagree with someone without becoming disagreeable?

What three pieces of advice come out of James 1:19 that would prove helpful when someone disagrees with you?

1. _____

2. _____

3. _____

What advice about conflicts can you derive from Proverbs?

6:16–19 _____

_____

11:14 _____

_____

12:15 _____

_____

14:29 _____

_____

15:1 _____

_____

15:18 _____

_____

17:14 _____

_____

17:27 _____

_____

18:13 _____

_____

Living Insights _____

Jesus said, "Where two or three have gathered together in My name, there I am in their midst" (Matt. 18:20). But it seems like a modern paraphrase captures the current condition of many twentieth-century churches: Where two or three are gathered together in His name, there is disagreement.

How you handle disagreement will determine whether your relationships will turn out *de*structively or *con*structively . . . whether they tear down or build up.

Read through 1 Corinthians 14:1–26. What principle keeps recurring in the passage that helps minimize divisions?

_____

_____

Let's dissect another key passage and see what we can learn about this process of building up one another.

> Let no unwholesome word proceed from your mouth, but only such a word as is good for edifica-tion according to the need of the moment, that it may give grace to those who hear. (Eph. 4:29)

What would be some examples of things that might be classified as unwholesome words?

_____   _____

_____   _____

_____   _____

What are some examples of a word that is good for edification?

_____   _____

_____   _____

_____   _____

How are you able to discern what the need of the moment is?

_____

_____

_____

According to Ephesians 4:29, how does God dispense His grace to others?

_____

_____

_____

What is the Holy Spirit saying to you regarding the specific application of this verse to your life?

_____

_____

_____

_____

Write Ephesians 4:29 on a three-by-five-inch card and carry it around with you until you've memorized it. The echo of it in your thoughts will come in handy when a conflict arises with another person.

Chapter 10

GRACE: UP CLOSE AND PERSONAL

Selected Scriptures

Perhaps the greatest book ever written besides the Bible was *The Pilgrim's Progress*. This seventeenth-century classic, written by John Bunyan, has touched millions of lives since its publication.

The allegorical story traces the pilgrimage of a man named Christian as he journeys from earth to heaven, from sin to salvation. Along the way he encounters such friends as Evangelist and Interpreter. He also comes up against such foes as Despair and Legality.

In the earlier part of his journey, Christian travels with a heavy pack on his back that represents sin. Some of those who worked against him promised to relieve the burden, but none could—least of all Legality.

> This Legality, therefore, is not able to set thee free from thy burden. No man was as yet ever rid of his burden by him; no, nor ever is like to be: ye cannot be justified by the works of the law.[1]

Not long after encountering Legality, Christian comes to the home of Interpreter, who leads him to a large room full of dust. It had never been swept since the day it was built. Bunyan describes how the room finally came to be swept clean.

> Then he took him by the hand, and led him into a very large parlor, that was full of dust, because never swept; the which after he had reviewed it a little while, the Interpreter called for a man to sweep. Now, when he began to sweep, the dust began so abundantly to fly about that Christian had almost therewith been choked. Then said the Interpreter to a damsel that stood by, "Bring hither water, and sprinkle the room"; the which when she had done, it was swept and cleansed with pleasure.

1. John Bunyan, *The Pilgrim's Progress* (Old Tappan, N.J.: Fleming H. Revell Co., Spire Books, 1977), p. 26.

Then said Christian, "What meaneth this?"

The Interpreter answered, "This parlor is the heart of a man that was never sanctified by the sweet grace of the Gospel. The dust is his original sin, and inward corruptions that have defiled the whole man. He that began to sweep at first is the law; but she that brought water, and did sprinkle it, is the Gospel. Now whereas thou sawest that, as soon as the first began to sweep, the dust did so fly about that the room could not by him be cleaned, but that thou wast almost choked therewith; this is to show thee, that the law, instead of cleansing the heart (by its working) from sin, doth revive, put strength into, and increase it in the soul, even as it doth discover and forbid it, for it doth not give power to subdue. Again, as thou sawest the damsel sprinkle the room with water, upon which it was cleansed with pleasure: this is to show thee, that when the Gospel comes, in the sweet and gracious influences thereof, to the heart, then, I say, even as thou sawest the damsel lay the dust by sprinkling the floor with water, so is sin vanquished and subdued, and the soul made clean through the faith of it, and, consequently, fit for the King of Glory to inhabit."[2]

To cleanse the room of all its defilements it took grace. It still does.

Christian's original name was Graceless. The same thing could be said today of all of us who have become Christians, for before we came to know Jesus we were graceless. Having been graceless for so many years, are we living lives now that are full of grace? Has the grace of the Lord Jesus so permeated us as to produce a grace awakening in our lives?

If not, today's lesson will explore the process that can produce the necessary changes to make us more grace-conscious people.

The Process That Leads to a Grace Awakening

Having cleansed our hearts of the debris of inward corruption and the dust of sin's domination, God is now daily at work to

2. Bunyan, *The Pilgrim's Progress*, pp. 31–32.

awaken grace within us. His goal, as the following passages indicate, is to bring our character to a Christlike completion.

> And we know that God causes all things to work together for good to those who love God, to those who are called according to His purpose. For whom He foreknew, He also predestined to become conformed to the image of His Son, that He might be the first-born among many brethren. (Rom. 8:28–29)

> For I am confident of this very thing, that He who began a good work in you will perfect it until the day of Christ Jesus. . . . who will transform the body of our humble state into conformity with the body of His glory, by the exertion of the power that He has even to subject all things to Himself. (Phil. 1:6; 3:21)

> Do not lie to one another, since you laid aside the old self with its evil practices, and have put on the new self who is being renewed to a true knowledge according to the image of the One who created him. (Col. 3:9–10)

Under God's watchful eye, we are all engaged in our own pilgrim's progress. He is fashioning the clay of our lives into the kiln-baked, porcelain-finished image of Christ so that we might be like His Son, "full of grace and truth" (John 1:14). This process involves at least three things.

First: *It takes time.* Learning anything takes time. Learning to become models of grace takes years. Like wisdom, it comes slowly. But God, meticulous craftsman that He is, is in no hurry, because He is in the business of crafting character for eternity.

Second: *It requires pain.* As He gouges His fingers into the clay of our lives, it's uncomfortable at best. When the clay resists and becomes hardened to His efforts, the pain is even greater, for then He has to take out His hammer and chisel. Because He loves us and wants us to be like His Son, He chips away at our lives. His hammer is wielded for us, not against us. But the process still is a painful one.

Third: *It means change.* Being graceless by nature, we resist the hands of God as they try to mold us into what He wants us to be. Still His hands ever knead our clay to make it pliable. Change is inevitable because God does not tire or give up. Remember the verse? He who began a good work . . . *will* perfect it, *will* bring it to completion.

Some Everyday Examples of Claiming Grace

In C. S. Lewis' *Mere Christianity* we read:

> The real Son of God is at your side. He is beginning to turn you into the same kind of thing as Himself. He is beginning, so to speak, to "inject" His kind of life and thought . . . into you; beginning to turn the tin soldier into a live man. The part of you that does not like it is the part that is still tin.[3]

There are areas in all our lives that are "still tin." Five common ones are insecurity, weakness, abrasiveness, compromise, and pride. Maybe by bringing grace up close and making it personal, we'll be able to oil some of the stubborn tin that still clings to our lives. And maybe then those rusty spots will become transformed into flesh.

The Tin of Insecurity—Claiming the Grace to Be What I Am

In 1 Corinthians 15:9 Paul calls himself the least of the apostles and unfit to even be called an apostle because of his persecutory past. But instead of sinking in a sea of insecurity, Paul asserts with confidence that "by the grace of God I am what I am" (v. 10). In spite of Paul's past, in spite of his unfitness to bear the name "apostle," the grace of God made him fit.

The Tin of Weakness—Claiming the Grace to Learn from What I Suffer

Another struggle we all live with is our own human weakness. A suffering that medication doesn't relieve. A failure that prayer doesn't remove. Because we're human, we're subject to all kinds of maladies and malaises. Paul's thorn in the flesh is a case in point (see 2 Cor. 12:7–10). Prayer didn't remove the thorn. It was grace that enabled him to bear that thorn with contentment.

---

3. C. S. Lewis, *Mere Christianity*, rev. and enl. (New York, N.Y.: Macmillan Publishing Co., Collier Books, 1952), p. 148.

The Tin of Abrasiveness—Claiming the Grace to Respond to What I Encounter

This type of grace has to do with our responses to people. The tin in us tends to be abrasive, to snap back. But Paul instructs us that speech should "always be with grace, seasoned, as it were, with salt, so that you may know how you should respond to each person" (Col. 4:6). Our words should be timely, well-chosen, and tactful. Truth alone can be hard to choke down. Grace makes truth not only palatable but appetizing. Grace cushions our words so that the truth can be received without needless offense.

The Tin of Compromise—Claiming the Grace to Stand for What I Believe

When strengthened by grace, we can stand firm against compromising our principles (Heb. 13:9). Our tendency to compromise stems from trying to appear as something we're not. Grace strips away the tin and helps us to be ourselves so that when we speak of our faith it rings true.

The Tin of Pride—Claiming the Grace to Submit to What I Need

Pride is the stiff, unmalleable tin of our old nature that keeps us standing erect in the presence of God instead of falling down prostrate at His feet. If that's our spiritual posture, we will walk away from His throne empty-handed, because "God is opposed to the proud, but gives grace to the humble" (James 4:6; see also 1 Pet. 5:5; Prov. 3:34).

Christ: Our Model of Grace

As pilgrims of faith, we travel a road that is often steep and rocky. It helps to know that others have gone before us and pioneered the way. In his book *Thoughts for Life's Journey*, George Matheson talks about how discouraging the pilgrimage of faith can be and how essential it is to look beyond that rocky incline to those who have gone before us.

> My soul, reject not the place of thy prostration!
> It has ever been thy robing-room for royalty. Ask
> the great ones of the past what has been the spot of
> their prosperity; they will say, "It was the cold ground
> on which I once was lying." Ask Abraham; he will
> point you to the sacrifice of Moriah. Ask Joseph; he

will direct you to his dungeon. Ask Moses; he will date his fortune from his danger in the Nile. Ask Ruth; she will bid you build her monument in the field of her toil. Ask David; he will tell you that his songs came from the night. Ask Job; he will remind you that God answered him out of the whirlwind. Ask Peter; he will extol his submersion in the sea. Ask John; he will give the palm to Patmos. Ask Paul; he will attribute his inspiration to the light which struck him blind. Ask one more—the Son of Man. Ask Him whence has come His rule over the world. He will answer, "From the cold ground on which I was lying—the Gethsemane ground; I received My sceptre there." Thou too, my soul, shalt be garlanded by Gethsemane. The cup thou fain wouldst pass from thee will be thy coronet in the sweet by-and-by. The hour of thy loneliness will crown thee. The day of thy depression will regale thee. It is thy *desert* that will break forth into singing; it is the trees of thy silent *forest* that will clap their hands.[4]

George Matheson, John Bunyan, and the apostle Paul would all agree: We on earth are in the "robing-room for royalty." And the tailor's name is *grace*.

 Living Insights

Picture yourself as a tin soldier who is gradually turning into a real one. Every joint that moves, every surface that softens, every hair that grows is a new and unfamiliar experience.

That picture captures the process of God's grace at work in our lives, taking us from rigid, lifeless tin to soft, living flesh. But the transformation is painful . . . and it takes time.

Where are you in the process of transformation?

Describe how God is working with the tin of insecurity in your life.

_____

_____

4. George Matheson, *Thoughts for Life's Journey* (New York, N.Y.: Hodder and Stoughton, n.d.), pp. 266–67.

_____

_____

. . . with the tin of weakness.

_____

_____

_____

. . . with the tin of abrasiveness.

_____

_____

_____

. . . with the tin of compromise.

_____

_____

_____

. . . with the tin of pride.

_____

_____

_____

In which area do you most need a grace awakening?

_____

What needs to happen before that awakening can take place in your life?

_____

_____

What is the proud, "tinny" response to God's transforming work (see Isa. 45:9)?

_____

_____

What is the humble, pliable response (see Isa. 64:8)?

_____

_____

How can you humbly submit yourself before the almighty molding power of God's hand (see 1 Pet. 5:6–7)?

_____

_____

 Living Insights STUDY TWO

If you were walking a treacherous path, would you rather have road signs along the way or a personal guide to walk with you hand in hand, one who knew every twist and turn of the terrain?

Road signs are similar in function to the way the Law directs us. A personal guide, on the other hand, is the way we are led when we are guided by grace. Dr. Paul Tournier notes the distinction between the two in his book *Guilt and Grace.*

> What is so narrowing, oppressive and deadly about the Law or about a moral code is that it is a thing. To rest upon it is to rest upon a thing and not upon a person. But the entire message of the Bible is that God is alive, He is a person, and He calls us into a living and personal relationship with Himself. A law commands and prohibits—and prohibits more than

it commands. A person speaks, inspires, directs, understands, leads continuously to deeper and more discerning perceptions, and produces a shift from the formal system of acts to the more penetrating system of motivation. . . .

This, then, is the secret: a personal encounter with God. It brings a much greater severity with oneself and at the same time a liberation from morbid scruples. Life becomes a joyous adventure which is endlessly renewed.[5]

Pilgrim, how is your progress? How are you faring on the upward climb of faith? A little disoriented, wondering which fork in the road to take? A little discouraged, aching from the burden of legalistic standards strapped to your back?

You don't need more road signs. You need to take the hand of the trailblazer of our faith, the Lord Jesus Christ. Won't you spend some time now praying for a more personal, more intimate encounter with Him? It will change your life . . . and it will turn your cumbersome climb into "a joyous adventure."

5. Paul Tournier, *Guilt and Grace,* trans. Arthur W. Heathcote (San Francisco, Calif.: Harper and Row, Publishers, 1962), pp. 167–68.

Chapter 11

ARE YOU REALLY A MINISTER OF GRACE?

Selected Scriptures

This chapter is dedicated to all of you who serve some segment of the body of Christ on a consistent basis. Perhaps you're a Sunday school teacher, an elder, a deacon, or a musician. Whatever capacity you serve in, this lesson is tailor-made for you.

To begin, we need to ask a crucial question: Are you a minister of grace?

Many other questions stream from this fountainhead to wash away the cosmetic exterior that may be hiding your true self: Are the people you serve given the freedom to be who they are, or do they feel pressured to live up to your set of expectations? Do you let others go, or do you smother them with control? Do people you minister to feel intimidated or relieved in your presence? Are you cultivating spontaneous, creative celebrants or fearful captives? Do you encourage those to whom you minister, or do you discourage them?

These surging questions can knock the wind out of you, but before you catch your breath, we need to ask a few more. Do you model grace in your own life? Is your work energized by your own strength and charisma? Is your agenda hidden? Are your motives pure and proper? Do you exploit those to whom you minister? Is yours a "grace awakening" ministry?

A Powerful Message from a Spirit-Directed Prophet

To help you appreciate the value of being a minister of grace, we want to introduce you to one of the most obscure men in the Bible—Zechariah.

Historical Background

At the time of Zechariah, Jerusalem lay in ruins. Her protective wall had been reduced to rubble. Her houses had been routed. Her temple had been razed. After living seventy years in captivity, her citizens had returned and had begun rebuilding the temple under Zerubbabel's leadership. But reconstruction of the temple had not progressed beyond the foundation phase for fifteen years because of opposition from Israel's enemies.

With passionate and often blunt rebukes, the prophet Haggai turned the people's attention to the unfinished temple. Zechariah shared the same vision as Haggai, but he spoke in a completely different style. His approach was a complementary one of grace.

A Timeless Reminder

The catalyst to Zechariah's message came in the form of a vision, recorded in Zechariah 4:1–5.

> Then the angel who was speaking with me returned, and roused me as a man who is awakened from his sleep. And he said to me, "What do you see?" And I said, "I see, and behold, a lampstand all of gold with its bowl on the top of it, and its seven lamps on it with seven spouts belonging to each of the lamps which are on the top of it; also two olive trees by it, one on the right side of the bowl and the other on its left side." Then I answered and said to the angel who was speaking with me saying, "What are these, my lord?" So the angel who was speaking with me answered and said to me, "Do you not know what these are?" And I said, "No, my lord."

As Zechariah rubbed the sleep from his eyes, the angel interpreted this rousing revelation for him. The word was for a weary and discouraged Zerubbabel, the governor whose task it was to complete the temple.

> Then he answered and said to me, "This is the word of the Lord to Zerubbabel saying, 'Not by might nor by power, but by My Spirit,' says the Lord of hosts. 'What are you, O great mountain? Before Zerubbabel you will become a plain; and he will bring forth the top stone with shouts of "Grace, grace to it!"'" (vv. 6–7)

The reconstruction project loomed before Zerubbabel like the sheer face of Mount Everest. And he had few volunteers willing to make the arduous climb. The new generation was simply apathetic, and the old generation was simply too tired from rebuilding the wall.

The words of grace in verses 6–7 must have come like a cup of cold water to Zerubbabel's weary soul. It must have taken a big burden off his back to learn that the responsibility for completing the temple was not the governor's but God's.

Theodore Laetsch, in his thorough work on the Minor Prophets, comments on verse 6.

> The two Hebrew words for "might" and "power" denote inner strength, . . . inherent power, courageous bravery, fortitude, as well as manpower, large numbers of soldiers, riches, leaders, well co-ordinated organizations, good financial systems, etc. The Lord's work, the building of His Temple, the inner growth, the expansion of His Church cannot be properly carried out by mere external means. Human strength and wisdom alone will fail. My Spirit must do it![1]

God's best work is not going to be done by human might or fleshly power. Our tendency, however, is to rely on our own strength. After all, cracking the whip does get results—just ask Pharaoh. But our blueprint for building shouldn't come from Egypt. It should come from heaven. From foundation to capstone, the temple was to be erected by grace, and grace alone.

How about the things that you're building? Are you relying on human might and power? Or are you relying on God's Spirit? Do you keep coming back to Egypt for advice when you run into a snag? What will it take to bring you back to a by-grace-alone style of ministry?

A Strong Warning

Every project you undertake can be accomplished your way or God's way. And sometimes only God can see the difference. Externally, it may look like God did the work; but internally, if it's initiated by your motives and completed by your strength, it's your work. It stands as a monument to you, not to God. There is no glory vertically, and there is no grace horizontally. Nor is there any satisfaction. Human strength is impressive, logical, and it works. But satisfaction is elusive; the only echoes from the hollow ring of human success are pride and guilt.

---

1. Theodore Laetsch, *Bible Commentary: The Minor Prophets* (St. Louis, Mo.: Concordia Publishing House, 1956), p. 428.

The great pastor of grace, Charles Haddon Spurgeon, says this about a pastor who operates in the flesh.

> A graceless pastor is a blind man elected to a professorship of optics, philosophising upon light and vision, discoursing upon and distinguishing to others the nice shades and delicate blendings of the prismatic colours, while he himself is absolutely in the dark! He is a dumb man elevated to the chair of music; a deaf man fluent upon symphonies and harmonies! He is a mole professing to educate eaglets; a limpet elected to preside over angels. . . .
>
> . . . Moreover, when a preacher is poor in grace, any lasting good which may be the result of his ministry, will usually be feeble and utterly out of proportion with what might have been expected.[2]

Two characteristics—the first concerning projects and the second, people—stand out in those who operate in the effort of the flesh rather than in the energy of grace. First, *those who operate in the flesh use human might in order to accomplish visible projects.* They import strategies from the world in order to make an impression; they adapt secular managerial styles to manipulate things in their favor.

Second, *those with a might-and-power style rely on personality power to get their way with people.* They rely on charisma rather than character, schemes rather than service, embarrassing others rather than setting an example for others to follow.

But when we restrain our own might and power and give the Spirit room to work, all the glory goes to God, and we get a satisfaction that nothing else can replicate.

Some Obvious Marks of a Grace-Oriented Minister

Several centuries after Zechariah's prophecy, we come upon the living temple of the New Testament church. Here we find several more characteristics of those who are truly ministers of grace.

One of those characteristics is *generosity with personal possessions.* In the first century, when the cradle of the infant church was first rocked, generosity festooned the fellowship hall.

---

2. C. H. Spurgeon, *Lectures to My Students* (1954; reprint, Grand Rapids, Mich.: Zondervan Publishing House, 1969), pp. 9–10, 8.

> And the congregation of those who believed
> were of one heart and soul; and not one of them
> claimed that anything belonging to him was his
> own; but all things were common property to them.
> And with great power the apostles were giving wit-
> ness to the resurrection of the Lord Jesus, and abun-
> dant grace was upon them all. For there was not a
> needy person among them, for all who were owners
> of land or houses would sell them and bring the
> proceeds of the sales, and lay them at the apostles'
> feet; and they would be distributed to each, as any
> had need. (Acts 4:32–35)

This abundance of grace prompted an outpouring of generosity.
And the result? "There was not a needy person among them"! An
atmosphere of grace is characterized by an absence of selfishness.
After all, freely we have received, so freely we should give (see
Matt. 10:8b).

A second characteristic of a grace-oriented minister is *encouragement in unusual settings*. Grace is what keeps a person flexible and
willing to adapt. One of the adaptations the Jerusalem church had
to undergo was taking the gospel beyond strictly Jewish racial
boundaries to reach the Gentiles. Acts 11:19–23 records the first
baby steps of the infant church in that direction.

> So then those who were scattered because of the
> persecution that arose in connection with Stephen
> made their way to Phoenicia and Cyprus and Antioch,
> speaking the word to no one except to Jews alone.
> But there were some of them, men of Cyprus and
> Cyrene, who came to Antioch and began speaking
> to the Greeks also, preaching the Lord Jesus. And
> the hand of the Lord was with them, and a large
> number who believed turned to the Lord. And the
> news about them reached the ears of the church at
> Jerusalem, and they sent Barnabas off to Antioch.
> Then when he had come and witnessed the grace
> of God, he rejoiced and began to encourage them
> all with resolute heart to remain true to the Lord.

Instead of an all-Jewish congregation, Barnabas saw a church
filled with Gentiles praising the Savior. He saw grace at work, and

he applauded it. And he modeled grace in his response of adapting and giving encouragement in what was for him an unusual situation.

A third mark of grace is *a life that's lived beyond the letter of the law.* A grace-awakened minister doesn't bash believers with the Bible or wag a dogmatic finger at the people in the pews. The minister of grace is one living under the freedom of the new covenant—not under the constraints of the old.

> Not that we are adequate in ourselves to consider any-thing as coming from ourselves, but our adequacy is from God, who also made us adequate as servants of a new covenant, not of the letter, but of the Spirit; for the letter kills, but the Spirit gives life. (2 Cor. 3:5–6)

The ministry of grace, according to Paul, doesn't depend upon our own adequacy (2:16b, 3:5), but upon authenticity (2:17). It emphasizes personal relationships (3:1–4) and exhibits the importance of a servant mentality (3:6).

It's important to be committed to the truth of God's Word, but that must be balanced with grace toward people. Our goal is not to be faster than a computerized concordance; our goal is to be like Jesus, full of grace and truth (John 1:14, 17).

The fourth characteristic of a grace-oriented minister is *liberty for creative expression.* Paul writes in 2 Corinthians 3:17,

> Now the Lord is the Spirit; and where the Spirit of the Lord is, there is liberty.

William Barclay illuminates Paul's words for us.

> He means that so long as man's obedience to God is conditioned by obedience to a code of laws he is in the position of an unwilling slave. But when it comes from the operation of the Spirit in his heart, the very centre of his being has no other desire than to serve God, for then it is not law but love which binds him.[3]

In your ministry do you really allow the freedom for creative expression? Do you restrict various forms of expression in worship, or is your love stronger than liturgy?

---

3. William Barclay, *The Letters to the Corinthians*, rev. ed., The Daily Study Bible Series (Philadelphia, Pa.: Westminster Press, 1975), p. 194.

The fifth characteristic of a grace-awakened minister is the ability to *release from past failures*. A grace ministry doesn't keep dredging up the past and slinging it in people's faces. Grace, like love, doesn't act unbecomingly and keep an account of wrongs. Instead, it throws a blanket of forgiveness over the past. See how Paul dealt with his own past in 1 Timothy 1:12–14.

> I thank Christ Jesus our Lord, who has strengthened me, because He considered me faithful, putting me into service; even though I was formerly a blasphemer and a persecutor and a violent aggressor. And yet I was shown mercy, because I acted ignorantly in unbelief; and the grace of our Lord was more than abundant, with the faith and love which are found in Christ Jesus.

Violence and blasphemy checkered Paul's past, but grace was available in such abundance that though his sins were as scarlet, they became white as snow (see Isa. 1:18). Consequently, when Paul talks about his past, he isn't airing dirty laundry; he's hanging out white linen for everyone to see the cleansing power of God's grace.

The same is true for us. No matter whether our past is stained with sexual sin, darkened by divorce, or discolored from addiction, the detergent of grace is tougher than any stain that soils our lives.

Marching Orders to All Ministers of Grace

Shortly before he died, Paul, the apostle of grace, urged Timothy, "My son, be strong in the grace that is in Christ Jesus" (2 Tim. 2:1). Model it. Teach it. Demonstrate it.

If we are to build the church that will withstand the heat in this life and the refining fire of judgment in the next, it can't be built by our own might and power. If it is, it will ultimately collapse under its own weight. If it is to stand the test of time and eternity, it must be built—from foundation to steeple—on truth and grace.

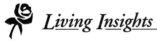 *Living Insights*   STUDY ONE

Are you a minister of grace? Let's personalize this question with which we introduced our topic for today. To help arrive at an answer, check the boxes below that apply to you.

I believe that . . .

☐ Having problems is sin.	☐ Problems are a part of my human condition. I can bring them to God and my fellow Christians.
☐ Emotions are sinful.	☐ Emotions are neither good or bad. It's what I do with them. "Be angry and sin not."
☐ A compulsive disorder is sinful.	☐ There is a difference between a compulsive disorder or disease and sinful behavior.
☐ Having fun is sinful.	☐ There are many different ways to delight in God's goodness.
☐ Spirituality equals perfection.	☐ We are to live within grace and not legalism.
☐ Sexuality equals sin.	☐ Our sexuality is a part of who we are as people and is to be enjoyed.
☐ Success (or its lack) is sinful.	☐ Prosperity or poverty is not due to deficient spirituality.
☐ Becoming a Christian fixes everything within me.	☐ Accepting Christ in my life enables and empowers me to face issues.
☐ If I am not healed it is a sin.	☐ Having illness is not due to my lack of faith.[4]

The more your check marks fell into the column on the left, the greater tendency you have toward being a legalistic person. If that's true of you, your spirituality is shame-based, relying on living up to the standards of others. If, however, your check marks fell more into the column on the right, you are a more grace-oriented person and have a healthier spirituality.

4. From "Shame-based and Healthy Spirituality" by Earl Henslin, as cited in *The Grace Awakening*, by Charles R. Swindoll (Waco, Tex.: Word Books, 1990), chap. 9. All rights reserved.

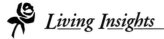

The angel's blueprints for rebuilding the temple in Zechariah 4:6 also give us the pattern whereby we can rebuild the demolished temples in our own lives.

Maybe you once had a sacred friendship that was razed by some devastating calamity or some crushing misunderstanding. Maybe you had a business go bankrupt and saw your dreams for the future turn into rubble. Maybe your marriage collapsed, and you fell, buried underneath tons of its debris. Or maybe the temple that was destroyed was the temple of your own body, ruined by drugs, illicit sex, overeating, or some other destructive influence.

Whatever the devastation, God can rebuild your life. How? The same way He prescribed the temple to be rebuilt—"Not by might nor by power, but by My Spirit."

In the space provided, describe the devastation of a temple of your own that weighs heavy on your heart, like Jerusalem's temple did on the heart of Zechariah.

_____

_____

_____

_____

_____

_____

What have you tried to do in your own might and power to rebuild it?

_____

_____

_____

_____

Has it worked? What was the result?

_____

_____

_____

What specific things could you do to step aside and allow God's Spirit to do the rebuilding?

1. _____

2. _____

3. _____

4. _____

Thumb through the pages of your memory to recall some biblical illustrations of people who tried to accomplish God-given goals by their own strength and ingenuity.

_____

_____

_____

What were the results?

_____

_____

_____

Now try to recall some examples of people who trusted in God and accomplished His purposes in the power of His Spirit.

_____

_____

_____

_____

_____

_____

What were the results?

_____

_____

_____

If your task is to trust God to do an impossible construction job in your life, your family, your job, or some other demolished area, remember—God delights in rolling up His sleeves for just such projects, because He "is able to do exceeding abundantly beyond all that we ask or think, according to the power that works within us" (Eph. 3:20).

Chapter 12

A MARRIAGE
OILED BY GRACE

Selected Scriptures

Actress Celeste Holm said, "We live by encouragement and die without it—slowly, sadly, angrily."[1] No matter if we're the CEO of a Fortune 100 company or just the night janitor who empties the wastebaskets, we all need encouragement. It's the oil that lubricates our soul and keeps it from grinding to a rusting halt.

The lack of encouragement is almost epidemic today. It's the reason people dread going to work in the morning. It's why kids can't wait to get out of school—and why some people can't wait to get out of a marriage.

What is it that enables us to give our mates this crucial encouragement? *Grace*—the lubricant that lessens the friction in marriage and keeps the gears of the relationship running smoothly.

No study on the subject of grace would be complete without addressing its importance in marriage. In today's lesson we want to focus on the essential value of grace in three areas of the husband-wife relationship: realities, responsibilities, and roles.

The Grace to Face Marital Realities

Let's turn our attention to 1 Corinthians 7, where we'll find three realities every married couple must face. The first is that *marriage requires mutual unselfishness.*

> Let the husband fulfill his duty to his wife, and likewise also the wife to her husband. The wife does not have authority over her own body, but the husband does; and likewise also the husband does not have authority over his own body, but the wife does. Stop depriving one another, except by agreement for a time that you may devote yourselves to prayer, and come together again lest Satan tempt you because of your lack of self-control. (vv. 3–5)

1. Celeste Holm, *Reader's Digest Treasury of Modern Quotations* (New York, N.Y.: Reader's Digest Press, 1975), p. 484.

Paul writes of "duty" and "authority" and "depriving" of one another. Contextually, these terms relate to sexual intimacy. But the application is much broader than that. The underlying principle in these verses has to do with unselfishness.

What does it take to operate in an intimate relationship unselfishly? It takes grace. Grace to accept, to overlook, to understand. Grace to forgive, to respect, to yield. Grace to affirm, to encourage, to give (see 1 Cor. 13:4–8a).

The second reality undergirding 1 Corinthians 7 is that *marriage means a lifelong commitment.*

> But to the married I give instructions, not I, but the Lord, that the wife should not leave her husband (but if she does leave, let her remain unmarried, or else be reconciled to her husband), and that the husband should not send his wife away. But to the rest I say, not the Lord, that if any brother has a wife who is an unbeliever, and she consents to live with him, let him not send her away. And a woman who has an unbelieving husband, and he consents to live with her, let her not send her husband away. (vv. 10–13)

The marriage institution was never designed for those whose first response is to drop out when the course load gets too heavy. So unless you are ready for a commitment that lasts for a lifetime, don't marry.

Paul's counsel in these verses couldn't be more emphatic. No less than four times does he take out his pen and underscore the permanency of the relationship (vv. 10, 11, 12, 13).

What does it take to form a permanent bond like that? It takes grace. Grace to go on, to realize that you sometimes aren't all your partner needs or wants or expected. The more grace there is in a marriage relationship, the more oil there is available to dissipate the heat caused by friction between the two partners.

There's yet a third reality that pops off the page of chapter 7: *marriage includes times of trouble.*

> I think then that this is good in view of the present distress, that it is good for a man to remain as he is. Are you bound to a wife? Do not seek to be released. Are you released from a wife? Do not seek a wife. But if you should marry, you have not sinned; and if a virgin should marry, she has not sinned. Yet such

will have trouble in this life, and I am trying to spare you. (vv. 26–28)

Every bride who thinks she's married a knight in shining armor had better stock up on polish, because the tarnish sets in quickly. And every groom who thinks he has married Wonder Woman—the perfect blend of Mother Teresa, Betty Crocker, Kristi Yamaguchi, and Whitney Houston—is in for a rude awakening.

Troubles are inevitable. Troubles that range from burnt toast to bedroom tiffs to big-time tragedies. And any one of these categories of trouble can capsize a marriage if grace isn't at the helm.

The Grace to Accept Personal Responsibilities

So much for the realities of the marriage relationship; now let's examine the responsibilities.

The Wife's Primary Responsibility

The wife's primary responsibility is to *know herself so well and respect herself so much that she is able to give herself to her husband without hesitation,* as Ephesians 5:22–24 instructs.

> Wives, be subject to your own husbands, as to the Lord. For the husband is the head of the wife, as Christ also is the head of the church, He Himself being the Savior of the body. But as the church is subject to Christ, so also the wives ought to be to their husbands in everything.

Many men have held these verses over their wife's head as a club. But a closer examination of the verses preceding this passage reveals not a dictatorial tone but a delicate one, resonant with harmony. There is an emphasis on being wise (v. 15), being filled with the Spirit (v. 18), overflowing with joy (v. 19), giving thanks (v. 20), and possessing a submissive spirit to one another out of respect for Christ (v. 21). If those things were as present in the marriage as they are in the context, the wife would have little difficulty giving herself unreservedly to her husband.

The Husband's Primary Responsibility

The husband's primary responsibility is to *love the Lord so deeply and to like himself so completely that he is able to give himself to his wife without conditions,* as Ephesians 5:25–30 indicates.

Husbands, love your wives, just as Christ also loved the church and gave Himself up for her; that He might sanctify her, having cleansed her by the washing of water with the word, that He might present to Himself the church in all her glory, having no spot or wrinkle or any such thing; but that she should be holy and blameless. So husbands ought also to love their own wives as their own bodies. He who loves his own wife loves himself; for no one ever hated his own flesh, but nourishes and cherishes it, just as Christ also does the church, because we are members of His body.

Again, grace is essential. It is the catalyst for chemical bonding to take place. Without it, the mixture of the sexes is at best unstable; at worst, it is explosive.

Dr. Kevin Leman notes the disparity between the roles that men and women assume when they marry.

Down through the centuries women have been the pleasers, men the controllers. . . .

Most women still do the giving, while the men continue to take. The woman is the one who is more capable of compassion, support, and being there when needed. Men still aren't in touch with their feelings the way women are. They are less capable of reaching out to make emotional contact. But they are very capable of reaching out to take whatever a woman has to offer, and in so doing, they often take advantage.[2]

The more grace-oriented a man becomes, the less he desires to control his wife. Grace doesn't crowd or stifle or suffocate; it allows room for growth.

When there is this type of grace-awakened love, the man loves his wife as he loves himself and the wife respects her husband. Which is exactly as God planned it.

Nevertheless let each individual among you also love his own wife even as himself; and let the wife see to it that she respect her husband. (v. 33)

2. Kevin Leman, *The Pleasers: Women Who Can't Say No—and the Men Who Control Them* (Old Tappan, N.J.: Fleming H. Revell Co., 1987), pp. 287–88.

The Grace to Fulfill Distinct Roles

We live in a day when roles within marriage have become blurred. The consequences can be seen in the home. Many a child grows up sexually confused, not knowing the significance of female femininity or male masculinity.

These blurred distinctions are brought into focus for us in 1 Peter 3.

The Wife's Role

Peter begins chapter 3 by writing to those wives whose husbands are indifferent about spiritual things.

> In the same way, you wives, be submissive to your own husbands so that even if any of them are disobedient to the word, they may be won without a word by the behavior of their wives, as they observe your chaste and respectful behavior. (vv. 1–2)

Remarkable. She wins her husband "without a word." How? Her life does the talking. If lived with grace, it speaks to him more eloquently and more poignantly than words ever could. And it is much more attractive than any external enticement could ever be. That's why Peter goes on to say,

> Let not your adornment be merely external—braiding the hair, and wearing gold jewelry, or putting on dresses. (v. 3)

Be careful not to use this verse in a legalistic way. It doesn't prohibit wearing jewelry any more than it prohibits wearing dresses. It simply means not to let your adornment be *merely* external. Finish the job by giving the proper attention to internals.

> But let it be the hidden person of the heart, with the imperishable quality of a gentle and quiet spirit, which is precious in the sight of God. (v. 4)

The wife's role, then, should be *to model true femininity, character traits that are precious to God and impressive to her husband.*

The Husband's Role

In verse 7, Peter turns the spotlight on the man's role within the marriage.

You husbands likewise, live with your wives in an understanding way, as with a weaker vessel, since she is a woman; and grant her honor as a fellow heir of the grace of life, so that your prayers may not be hindered.

The phrase "live with" means to "be at home with." The husband is not to just flop himself down on the couch, kick off his shoes, and nod off as he watches the nightly news. That's not the point of the verbal metaphor. The point is to know each other, to share, to make your mutual relationship a priority.

In fact, Peter goes further. He says, literally, "live with your wife *according to knowledge*." Really get to know her. Climb into her brain. See what she sees. Feel what she feels. Discover her most severe hurts and her most traumatizing fears. Uncover her hidden talents and her deepest joys.

Treat her as a weaker vessel, not emotionally or spiritually, but physically. Take care of her, help her, and respect the differences between you. In other words, be a masculine model of grace in your home. The husband's role, then, should be *to model genuine masculinity, unselfish and sensitive leadership that strengthens the home and gives dignity to his wife*.

On Being Heirs Together of the Grace of Life

We are also reminded in verse 7 that husband and wife are each "a fellow heir of the grace of life." Each of the key words in this verse has a special meaning. There is mutual equality—"fellow"; there is mutual dignity—"heir"; there is mutual humility—"grace"; and there is mutual destiny—"life."

If more marriages had this type of mutuality, there would be far fewer partners jumping the marital fence in search of greener pastures.

The echo of Celeste Holm's words, which began this chapter, comes back to us: "We live by encouragement and we die without it—slowly, sadly, angrily." If your marriage is failing, maybe it's because your mate is dying—from lack of encouragement, lack of affirmation, lack of respect . . . but most of all, from lack of grace, grace that only you can give.

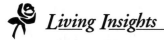 *Living Insights*

Dr. Willard Harley, Jr., has written a fascinating book titled *His Needs, Her Needs*. During his twenty years of marital counseling, he has discovered five basic needs women expect their husbands to meet and five needs men expect their wives to fulfill. By identifying them, we can more quickly and effectively oil any squeaky wheels with grace.

Five Major Needs of Women	Five Major Needs of Men
1. Affection	1. Sexual fulfillment
2. Conversation	2. Recreational companionship
3. Honesty and openness	3. An attractive spouse
4. Financial support	4. Domestic support
5. Family commitment	5. Admiration[3]

Dr. Harley states that the key need for the woman is affection—the feeling that she is truly prized, loved, and cherished. The key need for the man is sexual fulfillment.

If you were asked to list *your* five major marital needs in order of their importance, what would they be?

1. _____

2. _____

3. _____

4. _____

5. _____

On a zero to ten scale, ten being best, how well is your mate meeting need number one?

0   1   2   3   4   5   6   7   8   9   10

. . . number two?

0   1   2   3   4   5   6   7   8   9   10

---

3. Willard F. Harley, Jr., *His Needs, Her Needs* (Old Tappan, N.J.: Fleming H. Revell Co., 1986), p. 10.

. . . number three?

0 1 2 3 4 5 6 7 8 9 10

. . . number four?

0 1 2 3 4 5 6 7 8 9 10

. . . number five?

0 1 2 3 4 5 6 7 8 9 10

What could your spouse do in each of these categories to move those numbers up a notch?

1. _____
2. _____
3. _____
4. _____
5. _____

What do you think your mate's top five needs are?

1. _____
2. _____
3. _____
4. _____
5. _____

On a zero to ten scale, how well are you meeting need number one?

0 1 2 3 4 5 6 7 8 9 10

. . . number two?

0 1 2 3 4 5 6 7 8 9 10

. . . number three?

0 1 2 3 4 5 6 7 8 9 10

. . . number four?

0 1 2 3 4 5 6 7 8 9 10

. . . number five?

0 1 2 3 4 5 6 7 8 9 10

What could you do in each of those categories to move those numbers up a notch?

1. _____

2. _____

3. _____

4. _____

5. _____

If you're feeling brave, you might want to consider asking your mate to complete this exercise separately and then share and discuss your answers.

 Living Insights

The road to happily-ever-aftering together is potted with chuckholes. If we don't stop every so often to do a little road repair, we can knock the marriage out of alignment, blow a tire, or careen off the shoulder of the road.

What chuckholes do you find pitting your road to a happy marriage?

☐ Hurt feelings   ☐ Jealousy

☐ Anger   ☐ Self-image problems

☐ Resentment   ☐ Laziness

☐ Bitterness   ☐ Complacency

☐ In-law problems   ☐ Competing interests

Which is the most severe problem?

_____

Describe how this problem first started and how it's widened into the road hazard that it has become today.

_____

_____

_____

_____

_____

_____

_____

_____

Do you consistently pray about this problem?

_____

After talking with God about it, the next person you need to visit with is your mate. Sensitive issues like this are sometimes difficult to bring up, however, and even more difficult to communicate effectively. If you have trouble communicating about sensitive feelings, there's a book that you can read to help give you the skill and the confidence you may be lacking. It's called *The Language of Love* by Gary Smalley and John Trent.

A few helpful Scriptures you may want to consult are Matthew 5:23–24, Romans 12:17–21, Ephesians 4:26–32, and 1 Peter 2:21–23. They'll provide the road map to help you steer clear of the hazards that total so many marriages.

Chapter 13

THE CHARMING JOY
OF GRACE GIVING

2 Corinthians 9:3–8, 13–14; 2 Corinthians 8:1–9

Despite the elaborate decorations that deck the malls with wows and gollies, Christmas has a certain magic that manages to survive the crass commercialism festooning this most festive of holidays.

That magic has the power to soften the Scrooge in all of us, to turn our hardened "bah humbugs" into heartfelt "Merry Christmases." The magic of the season is wrapped up in a little package within our hearts called the joy of giving.

Giving scratches the itch of grace that lies just below our skin. It satisfies us and gives us pleasure to scratch, if only for a season. For many people, it is the closest they get to the grace of God— that grace which freely gives without thought of receiving in return.

Unfortunately, that effervescent joy of giving usually loses its fizz the day after Christmas. That is when we tend to revert to our old miserly ways and, for the next fifty-one weeks, we zip up our hearts and become defensive when it comes to giving.

What Makes Us So Dreadfully Defensive?

Whenever a preacher talks about giving, you can almost hear the groans ripple through the pews. Why? For several reasons, some of which are legitimate.

One: *It seems boringly repetitive.* Invariably, fund-raising is overstated and overdone. After a while, the droning on of the pastor or TV evangelist becomes monotone, and we block it out of our minds.

Two: *The whole thing has been commercialized.* Just as the meaning of Christmas can be lost among the ribbons and wrapping paper, so the joy of giving can be lost among the bar graphs and pie charts. Sometimes the whole fund-raising effort smacks of greed, tinseled with all kinds of techniques to motivate us to open our checkbooks. The goal of some ministries seems the same as that of the shopping malls—getting money from us.

Three: *There always seems to be a hidden agenda.* Comparisons are employed to show how much more we have than others . . . as if that should make anyone suddenly generous. The underlying

118

purpose? *Guilt.* Frankly, God is not concerned with *what* we give but *how* we give. Guilt as a motivator for giving has a numbing effect after a while, or else it turns us into compulsive givers devoid of joy. But once grace gets into your bloodstream, the pleasure of giving becomes addictive. Then the obligation from guilt will change to a compelling grace, and the focus will change from the amount of the gift to the attitude of the giver (see Acts 20:35).

What Makes Giving So Wonderfully Addictive?

The reasons for this healthy addiction are found in 2 Corinthians 8–9. You may remember the background to these two chapters. Behind Paul's remarks is a specific need. The mother church in Jerusalem had fallen on hard times. Unable to help themselves because of the depressed economy in Judea, the Christians there faced a bleak future. But that is not the case in Greece. So Paul challenges those in Corinth to participate in meeting this financial need.

At the beginning of his challenge, he mentions the generosity of the struggling churches in Macedonia, who gave—and gave gladly—even when their resources were scant. On the basis of their example Paul urges the Corinthians to reach into their pockets with the same zeal.

> Now, brethren, we wish to make known to you the grace of God which has been given in the churches of Macedonia, that in a great ordeal of affliction their abundance of joy and their deep poverty overflowed in the wealth of their liberality. For I testify that according to their ability, and beyond their ability they gave of their own accord, begging us with much entreaty for the favor of participation in the support of the saints, and this, not as we had expected, but they first gave themselves to the Lord and to us by the will of God. (2 Cor. 8:1–5)

Note that the Macedonians "first gave *themselves* to the Lord," then they gave their money. They gave during affliction. They gave in spite of their poverty. And they gave with great joy.

What makes this kind of giving so addictive? Four reasons from these two chapters stand out.

We Keep a Healthy Balance

But just as you abound in everything, in faith and

utterance and knowledge and in all earnestness and in the love we inspired in you, see that you abound in this gracious work also. (v. 7)

It's fairly easy to find a church where there is faith, good teaching, a working knowledge of the Christian life, zeal, and love. It's not so easy, however, to find generosity.

Generosity is a gracious work we are to abound in. Since we have freely received, we are to freely give (see Matt. 10:8b). When we do that, our lives maintain a healthy balance between what we take in and what we give out.

We Model the Same Grace of Jesus Christ

For you know the grace of our Lord Jesus Christ, that though He was rich, yet for your sake He became poor, that you through His poverty might become rich. (v. 9)

The Father didn't twist His Son's arm to leave heaven and come to earth. Jesus did it willingly. And when He offered Himself up on the cross, He wasn't prompted by obligation; He was prompted by grace. And by giving with grace, we more closely emulate the Savior.

We Counteract Selfishness and Covetousness

For it is superfluous for me to write to you about this ministry to the saints; for I know your readiness, of which I boast about you to the Macedonians, namely, that Achaia has been prepared since last year, and your zeal has stirred up most of them. But I have sent the brethren, that our boasting about you may not be made empty in this case, that, as I was saying, you may be prepared; lest if any Macedonians come with me and find you unprepared, we (not to speak of you) should be put to shame by this confidence. So I thought it necessary to urge the brethren that they would go on ahead to you and arrange beforehand your previously promised bountiful gift, that the same might be ready as a bountiful gift, and not affected by covetousness. (9:1–5)

Sometime in the past the Corinthians had promised to participate in an offering for Jerusalem. But for some reason they wavered in their commitment. Consequently, Paul prodded them to make good on their commitment and not to let covetousness get the best of them.

This grasping and grudging quality can all too easily gain a foothold in our hearts, can't it? When the raise takes effect or the tax refund comes in the mail, it's easy to let selfishness veto any previous pledges we had made. But when grace awakens in our hearts, it overshadows selfishness and greed.

We Become Increasingly More Generous

> Now this I say, he who sows sparingly shall also reap sparingly; and he who sows bountifully shall also reap bountifully. (v. 6)

These words articulate an important principle: The more we sow, the more we reap (see Prov. 11:24–25). We can't out-give God. We sow a grain, He blesses with a bushel (see Luke 6:38).

What Makes Grace So Attractive?

As Paul continues his discussion of giving in 2 Corinthians 9:7–14, four things reveal why grace is so attractive. The first is found in the first half of verse 7.

> Let each one do just as he has purposed in his heart.

The first reason grace is so attractive is that *grace individualizes the gift.* Underscore "each one" and "his heart." The emphasis is individual and personal. In an impersonal world, where individuality is often lost in the slush pile of statistics, grace giving distinguishes itself as being creatively fashioned in the innermost recesses of a person's heart.

The second reason grace is so attractive is that *it makes the action joyfully spontaneous.* The latter half of verse 7 says,

> Not grudgingly or under compulsion; for God loves a cheerful giver.

The word *cheerful* is a translation of the Greek term from which we get our word *hilarious.* So Paul is actually saying that God loves a hilarious giver, one who derives great joy from the act of giving, one who is as spontaneous in generosity as in laughter.

In his article "The Gift of Giving," Calvin Miller creatively illustrates the point of this verse.

I like the way the Magi gave their gifts, for they presumably returned "to the East" without expecting Mary and Joseph to give them anything in return.

Their gifts were meant for the baby Jesus, but there seemed to be no baby-shower obligation in their giving. . . .

Often at Christmas, gifts become a subtle power play, resulting in obligation. Such gifts may subtly say, "While my gift appears free, repay me in kind," or "Enjoy this, Joe, but you owe me one now." . . .

Let me suggest two ways to give a grace gift.

First, be sure it's impossible to measure the cost of your gift. My daughter's Italian mother-in-law has taught her to cook authentic Italian foods. So when my daughter wants to please me most, she fills a bowl with meatballs swimming in her marvelous marinara sauce, and I am content through long winters. . . .

Her love produces warm grace gifts from her pantry to which I could never attach a price tag. . . . Their real value is the way they show she loves and understands me.

Second, realize that non-material gifts are the best way to say, "Don't try to pay me back." . . .

One friend promised to pray for me all through the Christmas season. Another friend who knows I am fond of Shakespeare gave me a book of Shakespearean quotes from his personal library. . . .

. . . These gifts came with the assurance that Christ had prompted the gift and that it was given through Christ on the basis of our friendship. It was marvelous to see the Savior so involved in gifts that were not purchased, but given in the highest name of friendship.[1]

Verses 8–9 tell us of a third reason why grace giving is so attractive: *It enables us to link up with God's supply line.*

And God is able to make all grace abound to you, that always having all sufficiency in everything, you

---

1. Calvin Miller, "The Gift of Giving," *Moody Monthly*, December 1988, pp. 23–25.

may have an abundance for every good deed; as it
is written,

"He scattered abroad, he gave to the poor,
His righteousness abides forever."

When we possess an attitude of grace, we give . . . freely, spontaneously, generously, and sincerely. We give both ourselves and our material resources. That type of hilarious giving links us to the divine bank of heavenly resources. Its supply is inexhaustible. There is no good deed we can sign our name to that God can't cover the check.

A fourth reason why grace is so attractive is that *it leads to incomparable results*.

Because of the proof given by this ministry they will glorify God for your obedience to your confession of the gospel of Christ, and for the liberality of your contribution to them and to all, while they also, by prayer on your behalf, yearn for you because of the surpassing grace of God in you. (vv. 13–14)

Three incomparable results drip luxuriantly from these verses. First, others give God the glory. Second, these others learn by example to be generous. Third, the relationship that is formed transcends any gift we give.

What Makes Christ So Superlative?

The apostle of grace concludes this section with the words,

Thanks be to God for His indescribable gift! (v. 15)

When this thoroughly educated man—whose vocabulary was prodigious—thumbed through his mental dictionary, he found himself at a loss for words. The only word he could use was—*indescribable*. Why? Because it represents God's love gift to the world (John 3:16)— a gift that not only lies beyond words but beyond the realm of our understanding. That indescribable gift came wrapped in swaddling clothes almost two thousand years ago. And when the young Savior's eyes first opened, grace awakened and smiled on the world.

But the giving doesn't stop there. He gives us grace upon grace.

He who did not spare His own Son, but delivered Him up for us all, how will He not also with Him freely give us all things? (Rom. 8:32)

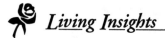 *Living Insights*

Look up these passages and jot down the principles about giving that you derive.

Guidelines for Giving

Proverbs 3:9 _____

_____

Proverbs 3:27 _____

_____

Matthew 6:1–4 _____

_____

Matthew 10:8 _____

_____

Luke 3:11 _____

_____

Acts 20:35 _____

_____

1 Corinthians 16:2 _____

_____

2 Corinthians 9:6 _____

_____

2 Corinthians 9:7 _____

_____

Ephesians 4:28 _____

_____

Benefits of Giving

Proverbs 11:25 _____

_____

Proverbs 22:9 _____

_____

Luke 6:35 _____

_____

Luke 6:38 _____

_____

Luke 14:13–14 _____

_____

1 Timothy 6:18–19 _____

_____

🌹 *Living Insights* _____ STUDY TWO

The story of the Good Samaritan in Luke 10:30–37 is a study in grace giving. In the story, the priest and Levite were religious people, yet they were the least responsive to the plight of the man who lay on the threshold of death. What was lacking in their lives that enabled them to look away without a twinge of conscience?

_____

How significant were their lives without this quality (see 1 Cor. 13:1–3)?

_____

_____

_____

List some of the gracious ways in which the Samaritan gave to the wounded man.

_____   _____

_____   _____

The application of the story is for us to follow the example of the Samaritan in showing mercy to those who need it, regardless of the cost, regardless of whether or not that cost will be reimbursed. How does living like that reflect God (see Luke 6:34–36)?

_____

_____

_____

_____

The following verses are good motivators for developing a grace-giving lifestyle. Take some time now to look them up, then write down the ideas that are helpful to you.

Deuteronomy 15:7–11 _____

_____

Proverbs 14:31 _____

_____

Proverbs 19:17 _____

_____

Proverbs 21:13 _____

_____

Proverbs 28:27 _____

_____

Matthew 25:31–46 _____

_____

Chapter 14

GRACE: IT'S *REALLY* ACCEPTING

Selected Scriptures

G race not only gives with joyful generosity, but it *receives* with grateful humility. When a person truly experiences a grace awakening, there is not only a desire to encourage, affirm, and support others, there is also an accepting attitude that allows others to reciprocate.

As easy and simple as this may sound, it is neither. It cuts across the grain of our natural tendency to be independent and invulnerable. We want to be people who pull ourselves up by our own bootstraps rather than people who have to reach out for an extended hand to be helped to our feet.

For many of us, the grace of giving comes naturally; it's the receiving end of grace that we have difficulty with. If this describes you, today's lesson should awaken a whole new dimension in your life.

The Flip Side of Several Strengths

Self-reliant people often have a strong commitment to character. But those who believe so firmly in the pursuit of character often forget that such pursuits can sometimes have a downside. Four problems come readily to mind.

First: *With a commitment to excellence there can come an attitude of intolerance.* There is nothing wrong with fighting mediocrity, but the casualties often become the very people within our ranks who are fighting by our sides. When we make perfection our standard— instead of accepting another's best—we become unrealistic in our expectations, forgetting the propensity in all of us humans to err.

Second: *With a lifestyle of discipline there can come impatience and the tendency to judge.* Those who have disciplined themselves against overeating have little patience with those with a Burger King belt line. And those who exercise diligently have little patience for those who get winded just trying to bend over and tie their Nikes.

Third: *With a broad education and a love for culture and the arts, there can be a flip side of exclusive sophistication.* If opera, for example, is your thing, you probably recoil whenever you hear the twang of a country-western song. As aesthetically and emotionally satisfying as the cultural world may be, an air of sophistication and exclusivity often accompanies it.

Fourth: *With an emphasis on independence and high production, there is often the presence of pride.* If you are an independent worker, an independent thinker, or have become independently wealthy, chances are good that you have a great deal of pride. There's nothing wrong with standing on your own two feet, thinking for yourself, or working hard, but it can lead to an attitude of feeling like you don't need anyone else or resisting when someone reaches out to you.

Examples of Resisting and Accepting Grace

The Bible tells several stories of those who resisted grace and those who accepted it. Let's take a few minutes to examine them.

Two Old Testament Examples: Moses and Samson

Exodus 3 records the account of a man who resisted grace when it was offered to him. His name was Moses. As we meet him on this page of Scripture, he's an eighty-year-old man. He works for his father-in-law as a shepherd in a rugged region of Mount Sinai known as Midian. It was a place of obscurity, loneliness, stinging sands, and howling winds. As he gazes into the starlit night and watches a falling star, no doubt he reflects on his own meteoric fall from the grace of Pharaoh's palace. He had it all there at the palace— an unequalled education, unparalleled luxury, and unlimited power.

It was the flexing of that muscle—power—which led to a change in his fate. While a member of Pharaoh's court, Moses happened upon an Egyptian assaulting a Hebrew. He intervened and murdered the Egyptian. Tragically, Moses thought he could deliver the enslaved Hebrews by his own efforts. But human might was not God's ordained means to free His people. Fearful, Moses fled for his life. For forty years he withdrew to the wilderness. And for forty years God was silent.

Undoubtedly, Moses felt he had disqualified himself by dropping the divinely appointed baton that had been passed to him. In the desert he had found refuge from Egyptian revenge, but not from guilt and remorse. It is there in that guilt-ridden wilderness that the hounds of heaven finally caught up with him.

> Now Moses was pasturing the flock of Jethro his
> father-in-law, the priest of Midian; and he led the

flock to the west side of the wilderness, and came to Horeb, the mountain of God. And the angel of the Lord appeared to him in a blazing fire from the midst of a bush; and he looked, and behold, the bush was burning with fire, yet the bush was not consumed. So Moses said, "I must turn aside now, and see this marvelous sight, why the bush is not burned up." When the Lord saw that he turned aside to look, God called to him from the midst of the bush, and said, "Moses, Moses!" And he said, "Here I am." Then He said, . . . "I am the God of your father, the God of Abraham, the God of Isaac, and the God of Jacob." Then Moses hid his face, for he was afraid to look at God. And the Lord said, "I have surely seen the affliction of My people who are in Egypt, and have given heed to their cry because of their taskmasters, for I am aware of their sufferings. . . . Furthermore, I have seen the oppression with which the Egyptians are oppressing them. Therefore, come now, and I will send you to Pharaoh, so that you may bring My people, the sons of Israel, out of Egypt." (Exod. 3:1–10)

Do you hear what's in that voice, radiating from the fire? It's grace, coming from God's merciful heart. Like the bush that kept burning, grace keeps reaching.

F. B. Meyer writes eloquently of this moment.

There are days in all lives which come unannounced, unheralded; no angel faces look out of heaven; no angel voices put us on our guard: but as we look back on them in after years, we realize that they were the turning points of existence. . . . It was so with Moses. . . .

. . . Suddenly, a common bush began to shine with the emblem of Deity; and from its heart of fire the voice of God broke the silence of the ages in words that fell on the shepherd's ear like a double-knock: "Moses, Moses."

And from that moment all his life was altered. The door which had been so long in repairing was suddenly put on its hinges again and opened.[1]

If you think Moses jumped at the chance to return to God's calling, you don't understand the grip of guilt. Four times he resisted the call: "Who am I . . . ?" (3:11), "What shall I say . . . ?" (3:13), "What if they will not believe me . . . ?" (4:1), "Please, Lord, I have never been eloquent . . . for I am slow of speech and slow of tongue" (4:10).

As Moses stammered around, God assured him that He would give him grace equal to the task. He assured the insecure Moses of His presence (3:12), His power (v. 20), His provision (vv. 21–22), and His guidance (4:12).

From Moses' response to God we learn an important thing about grace: *We resist grace when our guilt and shame have not been adequately dealt with.* The past dogged Moses' heels so relentlessly that he couldn't receive the grace God had offered him. He felt unworthy.

Of course, no one is deserving of God's grace. No one is adequate to receive it. But God gives it anyway. And that's the crowning majesty of grace.

The next example is of someone who accepted God's grace — Samson. He was set apart before birth to deliver Israel from the death grip of the Philistines (Judg. 13:5). If ever there was a life scripted for success, it was Samson's. His parents were strong believers who dedicated him to the Lord with the vow of the Nazarite — never was he to drink alcoholic beverages, to touch the carcass of anything dead, or to cut his hair.

We read in Judges 15:20 that Samson did indeed become successful: "He judged Israel twenty years in the days of the Philistines." For two continuous decades Samson proved faithful to his calling.

But then something went tragically wrong with Samson's life. While away from the home folks, Samson allowed his lust free rein by getting involved with a prostitute (16:1). Shortly thereafter, we find him in the valley of Sorek, Philistine country, his curls being stroked in the lusty lap of Delilah (v. 4). One night after he fell asleep, the conspiratorial Delilah motioned to her cohorts to enter the room and shave his head (vv. 18–19). That's when his herculean strength left him, and he awoke to find himself at their mercy.

Then the Philistines seized him and gouged out his

---

1. F. B. Meyer, *Moses, the Servant of God* (New York, N.Y.: Fleming H. Revell Co., 1950), pp. 39–40.

eyes; and they brought him down to Gaza and bound him with bronze chains, and he was a grinder in the prison. (v. 21)

Samson was a victim of his own lust, sentenced to live out his life in hard labor. He was a striking illustration of Proverbs 5:22, "held with the cords of his sin."

Though Samson reaped what he had sown, God's grace proved even more abundant than the moral crop failure in this man's life. Samson's hair began to grow, and with it, his strength (Judg. 16:22). Once he felt the power of God rippling through his muscles, another thing returned—the determination to fulfill his call of delivering Israel from the Philistines. After his captors brought Samson out of prison for sport, the broken man lifted up his eyes to heaven for grace.

Then Samson called to the Lord and said, "O Lord God, please remember me and please strengthen me just this time, O God, that I may at once be avenged of the Philistines for my two eyes." And Samson grasped the two middle pillars on which the house rested, and braced himself against them, the one with his right hand and the other with his left. And Samson said, "Let me die with the Philistines!" And he bent with all his might so that the house fell on the lords and all the people who were in it. So the dead whom he killed at his death were more than those whom he killed in his life. (vv. 28–30)

From the story of Samson emerges an important principle about receiving grace: *We accept grace when we release all our expectations.* When we no longer feel we deserve grace, but still extend our hands toward heaven, grace awakens within us. Samson's life was a washout, eroded by the flood of his torrential lusts. He didn't deserve a second chance. But that's when God shows Himself most radiantly, like the sun emerging from behind a dark billow of storm clouds. And that's when grace comes streaming down to bathe us in the warmth of its rays—when we least deserve it.

Two New Testament Examples: Peter and Paul

John 13 records a third story. The setting is an intimate one in an upper room. It is the last supper Jesus will spend with His disciples before He dies. He has much to tell them, especially about humility and service. But while He is formulating His sermon, the disciples are bickering over their respective greatness in the kingdom (see Luke 22:24–26). Instead of a sermon, Jesus gives them a visual aid that they would never forget.

> [Jesus] rose from supper, and laid aside His garments; and taking a towel, He girded Himself about. Then He poured water into the basin, and began to wash the disciples' feet, and to wipe them with the towel with which He was girded. And so He came to Simon Peter. He said to Him, "Lord, do You wash my feet?" (John 13:4–6)

The roomful of bewildered disciples sat and watched as the Son of God silently stooped to wash their feet. All, that is, except for Peter. When John recorded the event, the syntax of his sentence in verse 6 captured Peter's stunned reaction: "Lord, You, my, wash the feet?" We would smooth out the halting words to read, "Lord, are *You* planning to wash *my* feet?" Peter's response in verse 8 is emphatic in the Greek text:

> "*Never* shall You wash my feet!" (emphasis added)

In that moment of refusal we find a third principle about receiving grace: *We resist grace when our pride is still paramount.* Each time grace extends its hand, pride slaps it away. That's why grace and pride cannot coexist, because pride is resistant to the overtures of grace.

So far we've looked at three lives. Moses resisted grace because his guilt was not sufficiently dealt with. Samson accepted grace because his expectations had been done away with. Peter resisted grace because his pride was still paramount. Now we come to a fourth and final example—the apostle Paul.

Paul had much to boast about. He was "circumcised the eighth day, of the nation of Israel, of the tribe of Benjamin, a Hebrew of Hebrews; as to the Law, a Pharisee" (Phil. 3:5). Pretty impressive pedigree—at least in human terms. The list of accomplishments goes on: "As to zeal, a persecutor of the church; as to the righteousness which is in the Law, found blameless" (v. 6).

In the galaxy of the Jewish universe, Paul was one of the brightest luminaries—a star of the first magnitude. But when God looked at Paul's life then, all He saw was a black hole. It is God's estimation of Paul's life that caused the apostle to reevaluate his credentials: "But whatever things were gain to me, those things I have counted as loss for the sake of Christ" (v. 7). For years Paul had gone at warp speed in his zeal for righteousness. Only problem was, he traveled in the wrong direction, leaving him light years away from his destination.

What turned him around so that he could say, "Forgetting what lies behind and reaching forward to what lies ahead, I press on toward the goal for the prize of the upward call of God in Christ Jesus" (vv. 13b–14)? Grace is what steered him in that direction by enabling him to look at the map he was using in an entirely different light. He was now able to say that he "put no confidence in the flesh, although I myself might have confidence even in the flesh" (vv. 3–4a).

This brings us to a fourth principle about grace: *We accept grace when we no longer put confidence in the flesh.* By "flesh" we mean the tendency to achieve something in our own strength apart from trusting in the empowerment of God. When we put those things behind us, as Paul did, then we will be able to forge ahead to what lies before us—the magnificence of the Lord Jesus Christ.

What It Takes to Let Grace In

No matter how hard Jesus knocks on the door of our hearts or how persistently, that door must be opened from the inside (see Rev. 3:20). For some, that door has been closed for so long that the hinges have been rusted tight.

What can we do to oil those hinges and swing open that door? Two things.

First, it takes *an admission of humanity.* We've got to come to grips with the fact that we're only human, that we all sin and, sometimes, we sin greatly (Rom. 3:23). Second, it takes *an attitude of humility.* Nothing is so welcomed by grace as true humility, which is nothing more than a realization of one's true standing before God—that God is preeminent, that He alone is worthy of glory and praise.

A wonderful road lies ahead for those who *really* accept grace— a road that makes the yellow brick road to the Emerald City look like a footpath to the hay barn. It almost seems too good to be true. When George MacDonald, the great Scottish preacher, told one of his children about the glories of the future, the child interrupted and said, "It all seems too good to be true!" A smile spread across MacDonald's whiskered face as he answered back, "Nay, it is just so good it *must* be true!"[2]

2. Greville MacDonald, *George MacDonald and His Wife* (London, England: George Allen and Unwin, 1924), p. 172.

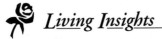

Before we can give grace to others, we first have to receive it ourselves (see 2 Cor. 1:3–4). But that's where the rub comes in. We're all enamored with being the Good Samaritan and giving grace to others. But none of us wants to be on the receiving end, as was the man who fell among thieves and was robbed, beaten, and left for dead (see Luke 10:30–37). If, however, we're ever to effectively extend a hand to others, we must first know what it's like to desperately clutch the hand that's extended to *us*.

Have you ever been there, on the receiving end of grace? Ever fallen among gossipy thieves who have robbed you of your dignity, your worth, your reputation? Ever been corporately dumped by the side of the road and economically left for dead, taken advantage of, used, and then crumpled up and discarded?

Describe such an incident in your life.

_____

_____

_____

_____

What form did God's hand of grace take?

☐ Physical help   ☐ Financial help   ☐ Spiritual help

Describe it. _____

_____

_____

_____

Did you receive or reject the hand of grace that God extended to you?

_____

What was it that prompted you to receive it or reject it?

_____

What did you learn from your experience to better equip you to extend grace to others?

_____

_____

_____

_____

🌹 *Living Insights* STUDY TWO

"Amazing Grace" is one of the church's most loved songs. It was written by John Newton, a man who knew about grace from firsthand experience. This is the story of his discordant life, and how grace reached down, picked him up, and put a new song in his heart.

> John Newton's mother, a Godly woman, died when he was not quite seven years of age. When his father remarried and after several brief years of formal education away from home; John left school and joined his father's ship, at the age of eleven, to begin life as a seaman. His early years were one continuous round of rebellion and debauchery. After serving on several ships as well as working for a period of time on the islands and mainland of the West African coast collecting slaves for sale to visiting traders, Newton eventually became a captain of his own slave ship. . . .
>
> On March 10, 1748, while returning to England from Africa during a particularly stormy voyage when it appeared that all would be lost, Newton began reading Thomas a Kempis's book, *Imitation of Christ*. . . . The message of the book and the frightening experience at sea were used by the Holy Spirit to

sow the seeds of Newton's eventual conversion and personal acceptance of Christ as his Savior. . . .

In a small cemetery of a parish churchyard in Olney, England, stands a granite tombstone with the following inscription: "John Newton, clerk, once an infidel and Libertine, a servant of slavers in Africa, was, by the rich mercy of our Lord and Savior Jesus Christ, preserved, restored, pardoned, and appointed to preach the Faith he had long labored to destroy." This fitting testimonial, written by Newton himself prior to his death, describes aptly the unusual and colorful life of this man, one of the great evangelical preachers of the eighteenth century.[3]

With that background in mind, meditate on your own past experience with the amazing grace of God. Then pray through the words of John Newton's song as if it were the new song that God had placed in your heart.

Amazing grace—how sweet the sound—
That saved a wretch like me!
I once was lost but now am found,
Was blind but now I see.

'Twas grace that taught my heart to fear,
And grace my fears relieved;
How precious did that grace appear
The hour I first believed!

Thru many dangers, toils and snares
I have already come;
'Tis grace hath brought me safe thus far,
And grace will lead me home.

When we've been there ten thousand years,
Bright shining as the sun,
We've no less days to sing God's praise
Than when we'd first begun.[4]

3. Kenneth W. Osbeck, *101 Hymn Stories* (Grand Rapids, Mich.: Kregel Publications, 1982), pp. 29, 28.
4. John Newton, "Amazing Grace," in *101 Hymn Stories*, p. 28.

BOOKS FOR PROBING FURTHER

The Great Awakening was a series of revivals that blazed through the American colonies between 1725 and 1760. One of the men who fanned those spreading flames was the evangelist George Whitefield, who was responsible for kindling evangelical Christianity in New England. He was used of God in a remarkable way. Lives were dramatically changed. Dead churches were resurrected. Missionaries were sent out among the Indians. Slavery was denounced. And great educational institutions, such as Princeton University, were established to educate a new generation of ministers.

Now it's time for another awakening—a *grace* awakening. We hope what you've read in this study guide has lit a fire in your life. And we hope the fire spreads—to your family, to your church, and to the nation in which you live.

If this series has sparked your interest for further study, you'll find some additional fuel for thought in the following bibliography.

Grace—A Biblical Perspective

Chafer, Lewis Sperry. *Grace*. 12th ed. Grand Rapids, Mich.: Zondervan Publishing House, A Dunham Publication, 1969. This biblical study on the topic of grace deals not only with the theological aspects of being saved by grace but with the practical aspects of living by grace.

Stedman, Ray C. *Authentic Christianity*. Portland, Oreg.: Multnomah Press, 1975. This practical exposition of 2 Corinthians 3–4 carefully distinguishes what it means to live under the new covenant of grace in contrast to the old covenant of the Law.

Grace—An Ecclesiastical Perspective

Hughes, Kent and Barbara. *Liberating Ministry from the Success Syndrome*. Wheaton, Ill.: Tyndale House Publishers, 1987. Just as some people are legalistically put on a performance basis and judged if they don't measure up, so also are churches. The authors show that success is not the standard God uses to evaluate a church, faithfulness is. Therein lies liberation, both corporately and personally.

Grace—A Psychological Perspective

Tournier, Paul. *Guilt and Grace*. Translated by Arthur W. Heathcote, J. J. Henry, and P. J. Allcock. San Francisco, Calif.: Harper and Row, Publishers, 1962. Though not thoroughly biblical in all his conclusions, the author does provide us with a warm, personal book that sheds valuable light on guilt and grace from a psychological perspective.

Grace—A Personal Perspective

Dobson, James C. *Love Must Be Tough*. Waco, Tex.: Word Books, 1983. When applying grace to personal relationships, especially the marriage relationship, many people think that means tiptoeing around the truth. Best-selling author and noted psychologist James Dobson says differently. What emerges from his study of marital conflicts is the principle of a *loving toughness* that is not only applicable to families in crisis but to healthy families as well.

Lutzer, Edwin W. *Failure: The Back Door to Success*. Revised edition. Chicago, Ill.: Moody Press, 1976. Failure is a reality that we all must face up to if we are to live authentic Christian lives. Lutzer's book shows us how to embrace our failures with grace and get them working for us instead of against us.

Seamands, David A. *Healing Grace*. Wheaton, Ill.: Scripture Press Publications, Victor Books, 1988. Many of us live with anxiety and defeat because grace has largely been a mental experience to us instead of a meaningful one. This distortion of grace stems from the twisted messages of a performance-oriented society, home, or church. In this book the author helps straighten out those distorted messages so that we can live liberated lives in vital union with God.

Smalley, Gary, and John Trent. *The Blessing*. Nashville, Tenn.: Thomas Nelson Publishers, 1986. The authors show how parental blessing, or lack of it, shapes our lives. They teach us how to forgive our parents when they have withheld blessing and also how to give it as a legacy to our own children. With grace as its primary motivation, the book offers hope for any who have never felt totally accepted and unconditionally loved.

Smedes, Lewis B. *Forgive and Forget: Healing the Hurts We Don't Deserve*. New York, N.Y.: Pocket Books, 1984. As Jesus forgave us, so we are to forgive others. For most of us, that's easier said than done. Smedes helps us work through the sometimes unfair pain of our past so that we may receive the grace not only to forgive but to forget as well.

―――. *Shame and Grace: Healing the Shame We Don't Deserve*. San Francisco, Calif.: HarperSanFrancisco; Grand Rapids, Mich.: Zondervan Publishing House, 1993. In this book, Smedes helps us differentiate healthy shame—that which warns us that we're becoming the kind of person we don't want to be; from unhealthy shame—a heaviness that burdens our spirits and crushes our joy in life. Grace, he has found, offers us healing and release, lightening our lives with a profound gratitude for living.

Some of these books may be out of print and available only through a library. For those currently available, please contact your local Christian bookstore. Books by Charles R. Swindoll may be obtained through Insight for Living. IFL also offers some books by other authors—please note the ordering information that follows and contact the office that serves you.

Ordering Information

The Grace Awakening
Cassette Tapes and Study Guide

This Bible study guide was designed to be used independently or in conjunction with the broadcast of Chuck Swindoll's taped messages which are listed below. If you would like to order cassette tapes or further copies of this study guide, please see the information given below and the order form provided at the end of this guide.

		U.S.	Canada
GRA	Study guide	$ 4.95	$ 6.50
GRACS	Cassette series, includes *all* individual tapes and bonus tape, album cover, and one complimentary study guide	46.75	54.00
GRA 1–7	Individual cassettes, includes messages A and B	6.00	7.48
GRASP	Special bonus cassette, includes messages A and B	6.00	7.48

Prices are subject to change without notice.

GRA SP-A: *The Grace Awakening: A 1996 Introduction*—
Selected Scriptures
B: *The Grace Awakening: A 1996 Epilogue*—
Selected Scriptures

GRA 1-A: *Grace: It's Really Amazing*—Selected Scriptures
B: *The Free Gift*—Selected Scriptures

GRA 2-A: *Isn't Grace Risky?*—Selected Scriptures
B: *Undeserving, Yet Unconditionally Loved*—
1 Corinthians 15:9–11; 2 Samuel 9

GRA 3-A: *Squaring Off Against Legalism*—Selected Scriptures from Galatians
B: *Emancipated? Then Live Like It!*—Romans 6:1–14;
1 John 1:9

GRA 4-A: *Guiding Others to Freedom*—Romans 6:15–23 and Selected Scriptures
B: *The Grace to Let Others Be*—Romans 14

GRA 5-A: *Graciously Disagreeing and Pressing On*—Acts 15:36–41; Ephesians 4:29–32
   B: *Grace: Up Close and Personal*—Selected Scriptures

GRA 6-A: *Are You Really a Minister of Grace?*—Selected Scriptures
   B: *A Marriage Oiled by Grace*—Selected Scriptures

GRA 7-A: *The Charming Joy of Grace Giving*—2 Corinthians 9:3–8, 13–14; 2 Corinthians 8:1–9
   B: *Grace: It's Really Accepting*—Selected Scriptures

HOW TO ORDER BY PHONE OR FAX
(Credit card orders only)

Internet address: http://www.insight.org

United States: 1-800-772-8888 or FAX (714) 575-5684, 24 hours a day, 7 days a week

Canada: 1-800-663-7639. Vancouver residents call (604) 532-7172, from 8:00 A.M. to 4:30 P.M., Pacific time, Monday through Friday FAX (604) 532-7173 anytime, day or night

Australia and the South Pacific: (03) 9872-4606 or FAX (03) 9874-8890 from 8:00 A.M. to 5:00 P.M., Monday through Friday

Other International Locations: call the International Ordering Services Department in the United States at (714) 575-5000 from 8:00 A.M. to 4:30 P.M., Pacific time, Monday through Friday FAX (714) 575-5683 anytime, day or night

HOW TO ORDER BY MAIL

United States
- Mail to: Processing Services Department
    Insight for Living
    Post Office Box 69000
    Anaheim, CA 92817-0900
- Sales tax: California residents add 7.25%.
- Shipping and handling charges must be added to each order. See chart on order form for amount.
- Payment: personal checks, money orders, credit cards (Visa, MasterCard, Discover Card, and American Express). No invoices or COD orders available.
- $10 fee for *any* returned check.

Canada

- Mail to: Insight for Living Ministries
  Post Office Box 2510
  Vancouver, BC V6B 3W7
- Sales tax: please add 7% GST. British Columbia residents also add 7% sales tax (on tapes or cassette series).
- Shipping and handling charges must be added to each order. See chart on order form for amount.
- Payment: personal cheques, money orders, credit cards (Visa, Master-Card). No invoices or COD orders available.
- Delivery: approximately four weeks.

Australia and the South Pacific

- Mail to: Insight for Living, Inc.
  GPO Box 2823 EE
  Melbourne, Victoria 3001, Australia
- Shipping: add 25% to the total order.
- Delivery: approximately four to six weeks.
- Payment: personal checks payable in Australian funds, international money orders, or credit cards (Visa, MasterCard, and Bankcard).

United Kingdom and Europe

- Mail to: Insight for Living
  c/o Trans World Radio
  Post Office Box 1020
  Bristol BS99 1XS
  England, United Kingdom
- Shipping: add 25% to the total order.
- Delivery: approximately four to six weeks.
- Payment: cheques payable in sterling pounds or credit cards (Visa, MasterCard, and American Express).

Other International Locations

- Mail to: International Processing Services Department
  Insight for Living
  Post Office Box 69000
  Anaheim, CA 92817-0900
- Shipping and delivery time: please see chart that follows.
- Payment: personal checks payable in U.S. funds, international money orders, or credit cards (Visa, MasterCard, and American Express).

Type of Shipping	Postage Cost	Delivery
Surface	10% of total order*	6 to 10 weeks
Airmail	25% of total order*	under 6 weeks

Use U.S. price as a base.

Our Guarantee: Your complete satisfaction is our top priority here at Insight for Living. If you're not completely satisfied with anything you order, please return it for full credit, a refund, or a replacement, as *you* prefer.

Insight for Living Catalog: The Insight for Living catalog features study guides, tapes, and books by a variety of Christian authors. To obtain a free copy, call us at the numbers listed above.

Order Form
United States, Australia, and Other International Locations
(Canadian residents please use order form on reverse side.)

GRACS represents the entire *The Grace Awakening* series in a special album cover, while GRA 1–7 are the individual tapes included in the series. GRA represents this study guide, should you desire to order additional copies. GRASP represents the special bonus tape.

GRA	Study guide	$ 4.95 ea.
GRACS	Cassette series, includes *all* individual tapes and bonus tape, album cover, and one complimentary study guide	46.75
GRA 1–7	Individual cassettes, includes messages A and B	6.00 ea.
GRASP	Special bonus cassette, includes messages A and B	6.00 ea.

Product Code	Product Description	Quantity	Unit Price	Total
			$	$

Amount of Order	First Class	UPS
$ 7.50 and under	1.00	4.00
$ 7.51 to 12.50	1.50	4.25
$12.51 to 25.00	3.50	4.50
$25.01 to 35.00	4.50	4.75
$35.01 to 60.00	5.50	5.25
$60.00 and over	6.50	5.75

Order Total	
UPS ❑ First Class ❑ *Shipping and handling must be added. See chart for charges.*	
Subtotal	
California Residents—Sales Tax *Add 7.25% of subtotal.*	
Non-United States Residents *Australia and Europe add 25%. All other locations: U.S. price plus 10% surface postage or 25% airmail.*	
Gift to Insight for Living *Tax-deductible in the United States.*	
Total Amount Due *Please do not send cash.*	$

Fed Ex and Fourth Class are also available. Please call for details.

If you are placing an order after January 1, 1997, please call for current prices.

Prices are subject to change without notice.

Payment by: ❑ Check or money order payable to Insight for Living   ❑ Credit card

(Circle one):   Visa   MasterCard   Discover Card   American Express   Bankcard (In Australia)

Number _____

Expiration Date _____   Signature _____

We cannot process your credit card purchase without your signature.

Name _____

Address _____

City _____   State _____

Zip Code _____   Country _____

Telephone (___) _____   Radio Station ____ ____ ____ ____

If questions arise concerning your order, we may need to contact you.

Mail this order form to the Processing Services Department at one of these addresses:

Insight for Living
Post Office Box 69000, Anaheim, CA 92817-0900

Insight for Living, Inc.
GPO Box 2823 EE, Melbourne, VIC 3001, Australia

Order Form
Canadian Residents

(Residents of the United States, Australia, and other international locations, please use order form on reverse side.)

GRACS represents the entire *The Grace Awakening* series in a special album cover, while GRA 1–7 are the individual tapes included in the series. GRA represents this study guide, should you desire to order additional copies. GRASP represents the special bonus tape.

GRA	Study guide	$ 6.50 ea.
GRACS	Cassette series, includes *all* individual tapes and bonus tape, album cover, and one complimentary study guide	54.00
GRA 1–7	Individual cassettes, includes messages A and B	7.48 ea.
GRASP	Special bonus cassette, includes messages A and B	7.48 ea.

Product Code	Product Description	Quantity	Unit Price	Total
			$	$

Amount of Order	Canada Post
Orders to $10.00	2.00
$10.01 to 30.00	3.50
$30.01 to 50.00	5.00
$50.01 to 99.99	7.00
$100 and over	Free

Loomis is also available. Please call for details.

If you are placing an order after January 1, 1997, please call for current prices.

Prices are subject to change without notice.

Subtotal	
Add 7% GST	
British Columbia Residents *Add 7% sales tax on individual tapes or cassette series.*	
Shipping *Shipping and handling must be added. See chart for charges.*	
Gift to Insight for Living Ministries *Tax-deductible in Canada.*	
Total Amount Due *Please do not send cash.*	$

Payment by: ❑ Cheque or money order payable to Insight for Living Ministries
❑ Credit card

(Circle one): Visa   MasterCard   Number _____

Expiration Date _____   Signature _____
We cannot process your credit card purchase without your signature.

Name _____

Address _____

City _____   Province _____

Postal Code _____   Country _____

Telephone (___) _____   Radio Station ____ ____ ____ ____
If questions arise concerning your order, we may need to contact you.

Mail this order form to the Processing Services Department at the following address:

Insight for Living Ministries
Post Office Box 2510
Vancouver, BC, Canada V6B 3W7